THE CONFEDERATE SOLDIER'S POCKET

MANUAL OF DEVOTIONS

INCLUDING BALM FOR THE WEARY

AND THE WOUNDED

COMPILED BY

CHARLES TODD QUINTARD

MERCER
UNIVERSITY PRESS

Endowed by
TOM WATSON BROWN
and
THE WATSON-BROWN FOUNDATION, INC.

THE CONFEDERATE SOLDIER'S

POCKET MANUAL OF

DEVOTIONS

INCLUDING BALM FOR THE

WEARY AND WOUNDED

COMPILED BY

CHARLES TODD QUINTARD

FOREWORD BY WILLIAM O. NISBET, JR.

INTRODUCTION BY SAM DAVIS ELLIOTT

MERCER UNIVERSITY PRESS
MACON, GEORGIA

MUP/P402

© 2009 Mercer University Press
1400 Coleman Avenue
Macon, Georgia 31207

First Edition.

978-0-88146-175-6

Library of Congress Cataloging-in-Publication Data

The confederate soldier's pocket manual of devotions including balm
for the weary and the wounded / compiled by Charles Todd
Quintard ; foreword by William O. Nisbet, Jr. ; introduction by Sam
Davis Elliott. -- 1st ed.
p. cm.
Rev. ed. of: Balm for the weary and the wounded. 1864.
Includes bibliographical references and index.
ISBN-13: 978-0-88146-175-6 (pbk. : alk. paper)
ISBN-10: 0-88146-175-X (pbk. : alk. paper)
1. Armed Forces—Prayers and devotions. 2. Soldiers—Religious
life—Confederate States of America. I. Quintard, C. T. (Charles
Todd), 1824-1898. II. Title: Balm for the weary and the wounded.
BV4588.Q56 2009
242'.68—dc22
2009025195

THE CONFEDERATE SOLDIER'S POCKET
MANUAL OF DEVOTIONS.
COMPILED BY REV. C. T. QUINTARD,
Chaplain 1st Tenn. Regiment.
CHARLESTON:
PRINTED BY EVANS & COGSWELL, NO. 3
BROAD STREET
1863.
[4234 (Rare Book Collection, University of North
Carolina at Chapel Hill)]

BALM FOR THE WEARY AND THE WOUNDED.
BY REV. C.T. QUINTARD,
Chaplain 1st Tenn. Reg't, C.S.A.
COLUMBIA:
EVANS & COGSWELL, PRINTERS.
1864.
[4235.1 Conf. (Rare Book Collection, University of
North Carolina at Chapel Hill)]

FOREWORD

Nurture the living.
Care for the wounded.
Honor the dead.
　　　　—The credo of the Army Chaplain Corps

Army chaplains first used this credo in the late 1980s. It summarizes over 200 years of chaplaincy ministry with soldiers during war and peace.

During the Civil War, Confederate chaplain Charles Todd Quintard compiled and published two booklets that capture the essence of this credo: *The Confederate Soldier's Pocket Manual of Devotions* and *Balm for the Weary and the Wounded.*

Dr. Charles Todd Quintard (1824–1898) was born in Connecticut and trained to be a medical doctor in New York. He moved to Georgia in 1847 to practice medicine, then to Tennessee. At the age of thirty, well established as a professor of physiology and pathological anatomy at the Memphis Medical College in Tennessee, he came under the influence of an Episcopal bishop and studied for the ministry.

A family biographer summed up the sort of army chaplain he would become, "…having made up his mind that a man's soul is worth more than his body, he determined to take orders in the Church." Six years later, the Reverend Quintard had become the rector of the Church of the Advent, Nashville, Tennessee. The respect he gained in his new hometown led to his election as chaplain of the First Tennessee Regiment.

In 1861 Chaplain Quintard marched off to care for his soldiers as they joined the Army of Virginia.

Over the next four years, he traveled with the Confederate army from Virginia to Tennessee to Georgia, where he finished his Civil War duty as a hospital chaplain. When his soldiers needed a surgeon, Quintard did not hesitate to take up his first vocation and care for their bodies: removing minié balls, amputating limbs, bandaging wounds.

But his primary calling was to nurture souls. As a chaplain, he counseled privates and generals. He preached to small groups and joined with other chaplains in worship and revivals in the open, in chapels or churches wherever the army paused, and in the hospitals. He evangelized officers and enlisted men. He provided comfort to the sick and the wounded. He ministered to those condemned to death for desertion. He was at the bedside of those dying of their wounds. He officiated at funerals and offered words of comfort to the families of those who died.

To provide for their spiritual uplift when he could not be physically present, Quintard published in 1863 *The Confederate Soldier's Pocket Manual of Devotions*. The manual draws heavily on the Episcopal *Book of Common Prayer*: morning and evening prayers, directed prayers, a litany and collects, the Creed and the Ten Commandments. Quintard changed the grammar of the church's prayer book from the plural to the singular to personalize the readings for the individual soldier. Half of the manual comprises forty-four hymns—many still familiar to churchgoers today.

These familiar forms of piety focused the heart and mind of the soldier toward God. Quintard's deepest desire was that the individual, once focused, would "live a sincere Christian life," "trust (his) God" and "look unto Jesus."

As one would expect of a chaplain in the Confederate army, Quintard included a brief prayer to "bless Thy servant, the President of the Confederate States." But Quintard's daily experiences with an Army in the field, hearing and sharing a soldier's hopes and fears, led him to write from a universal, human perspective. Faith, trust and devotion to God are themes even a Union soldier would have found comforting had he come into possession of *The Confederate Soldier's Pocket Manual of Devotions.*

As the war wore on, Quintard's thoughts were more and more with "our soldiers (who) have, by reason of wounds or disease, been compelled to exchange active service in the field for the harder and more wearying service in the hospital, or on the bed of sickness and pain."

Published in 1864, *Balm for the Weary and the Wounded* is dedicated to his wife's first cousin, Captain Thomas Edward King of Roswell, Georgia. King was so severely wounded at the First Battle of Manassas in July, 1861, that he was not fit to return to duty with his regiment. But when the Union Army entered Georgia two years later, he joined the staff of General Preston Smith. Both Smith and King died of wounds received at Chickamauga. Chaplain Quintard recovered his cousin's body from the field and officiated at the burial.

The tone of *Balm for the Weary and the Wounded* is reflected in its title. Fatigue, sickness, disease, wounds and death assault the human body and spirit. People become weary. Physical, emotional and spiritual wounds test one's faith, especially in the circumstances of war. Is there a purpose behind such suffering? Is there a balm capable of soothing the raw emotions and spirits of the wounded and crippled and of the widow and orphan?

In this second booklet, Quintard reached back often to the writers of the Oxford Movement, which was his theological underpinning. In addition to familiar prayers, collects, and hymns from the *Book of Common Prayer*, he adds poems, sermons, and religious texts of this movement. Quintard believes God's spirit provides that balm through the teachings and sacraments of the church, enabling the human spirit to prevail.

An acquaintance said of Quintard, "His heart was so tender and sympathetic, and his faith was so strong and entire, that his consolations were to the suffering and sorrowful a message from God." There is a timeless quality that still speaks in Quintard's booklets.

Where do individuals "soldier on" in life today? One person wears a uniform and serves with comrades in far-away places. Another is a first responder in the local community. Some are spouses, parents, or children of loved ones absent and in harm's way. Some are wounded and scarred physically, mentally, and spiritually by military combat. Some are wounded and scarred with addiction, despair, disease, or depression.

Whether in solitude or surrounded by others, there is human struggle common to all. All people fight against the "creatures" that the apostle Paul warns will attempt to separate the faithful from Jesus Christ: "tribulation or distress or persecution or famine or nakedness or peril or sword…death or life, principalities or powers, things present or things to come." (Romans 8:35–38)

Whatever your hopes and fears, you will find in these two books words of hope, strength, and perseverance that Chaplain Quintard shared from his own heart and soul with his soldiers and their families.

William O. Nisbet, Jr.
Marietta, GA
March 2008

William O. Nisbet, Jr., is a Presbyterian Church (USA) minister and a chaplain in the United States Army Reserve. He has been on active duty at Forces Command, Fort McPherson, Georgia, since the terrorist attacks of September 11, 2001. He is the great-great-grandson of Chaplain Charles Todd Quintard.

INTRODUCTION

The widely varied personalities of the Confederate Army of Tennessee are as much a part of its story as its long losing struggle to defend the Confederate heart-land. The grimness of General Braxton Bragg contrasts with the wry resignation of Private Sam Watkins. The elegant dignity of Leonidas Polk, a bishop and a mem-ber of the southern elite, stands out against the profane roughness of the uneducated Nathan Bedford Forrest, a comparison which demonstrates that education and refinement are poor indicators of military competence. The cautious Joseph Johnston is aptly juxtaposed with the impetuous John Bell Hood. Along with these men marched the military scientist William Hardee, the shy immigrant Patrick Cleburne, the quietly competent Alexander Stewart, and more politicians turned soldiers than seems imaginable.

Familiar to each of these men, high and low, was the chaplain of the First Tennessee Infantry, Charles Todd Quintard, who lent his own individuality to this highly volatile mix of proud men. Zealous as a priest, skilled as a physician, accomplished as a writer, effective as an organizer, as comfortable in his ministry to the men in the ranks as with officers and politicians, Quintard was an outstanding figure of tireless energy. An admiring bishop deemed the multi-talented chaplain as incomparable in his usefulness, a sentiment with which the men of the First Tennessee would have heartily agreed. In a significant way, Quintard was faithful to the officers and men of the Army of Tennessee to the end, as his contemporary diary and late in life recollections of the war are a valuable source for modern historians seeking to understand the personalities and events that defined the army.

Quintard was born in Stamford, Connecticut on December 22, 1824 in a family of comfortable wealth. Of French Huguenot descent, he was educated at Trinity School and Columbia College in New York City, and obtained a doctor of medicine degree from the University of the City of New York in 1847. After a year at the famous Bellevue Hospital in New York, he moved to Athens, Georgia and to begin a medical practice. While in Georgia, he met and married Eliza Catherine Hand, whose grandfather was wealthy industrialist Roswell King. In 1851, he accepted a position at the Medical College of Memphis, and moved to that city. During his time on that faculty, Quintard served as the co-editor of the *Memphis Medical Recorder*, a publication noted for its valuable contribution to knowledge of the diseases of the Mississippi Valley.[1]

---

[1] Charles Todd Quintard, *Doctor Quintard, Chaplain C.S.A. and Second Bishop of Tennessee: The Memoir and Civil War Diary of Charles Todd Quintard*, ed. Sam Davis Elliott, (Baton Rouge: Louisiana State University Press, 2003), 9-10;

While in Memphis, Quintard became friends with the James Hervey Otey, the Episcopal Bishop of Tennessee. Otey's influence proved a decisive turning point in the young professor's life, as in 1854 Quintard became a candidate for the priesthood. Ordained as a deacon in 1855 and as a priest in 1856, Quintard moved to Nashville to serve as rector of the Church of the Advent, and served that parish in addition to two others. On account of his singular ability to relate to young men, in 1859 a Nashville militia company, the Rock City Guard, named him their chaplain.[2]

Of northern birth, Quintard opposed the secession movement, and publicly and privately spoke in favor of the Union.[3] When Tennessee joined the Confederacy after the fall of Fort Sumter, however, he felt it was his duty to follow his adopted state out of the Union. The Rock City Guard became part of the First Tennessee Regiment, and its members "urgently pressed" Quintard to "accompany us throughout the campaign as our friend and spiritual advisor." Quintard accordingly sent his wife and two small children back to her family in Georgia, and departed for Virginia in August, 1861. Before joining his

---

"Miscellaneous Intelligence," *The American Journal of Science and Arts*, 2nd Series, 17(1853):303.

[2]Quintard, *Doctor Quintard*, 10-11.

[3]Although a Unionist, Quintard owned a slave boy in 1864-1865, and had a paternalistic view toward African-Americans. Ibid., 236, 257.

regiment in the field, Quintard diverted to Richmond for a few weeks to attend to his wife's cousin, Capt. Thomas Edward King, who was wounded at the battle of First Manassas.[4]

From that point, Quintard's Civil War experience was as wide and varied as that of any soldier or civilian. For the remainder of 1861, Quintard endured many of the hardships of the men of his regiment as they participated in the early campaigns in Virginia. Along the way, Quintard met Gen. Robert E. Lee, Maj. Gen. Thomas (Stonewall) Jackson, and other luminaries. As Quintard later wrote, he was tempted by Satan to leave his chaplaincy and join the staff of Brig. Gen. William W. Loring in early 1862, and in that capacity participated in the arduous Romney campaign that resulted in great enmity between Loring and Jackson. Quintard then transferred with Loring to southwest Virginia, stopping to visit with Jefferson Davis before arriving in Norfolk in time to see a skirmish between the *Monitor* and the *Virginia*.[5]

Meanwhile, the loss of large portions of Middle and West Tennessee as a result of the fall of Fort Henry and Fort Donelson in February, 1862 resulted in the transfer of the First Tennessee to its home state. Realizing that his leaving his role as a chaplain had been a mistake,

---

[4] Ibid, 10-11, 155.
[5] Ibid, 17-45.

Quintard resigned his post with Loring and was quickly reappointed as chaplain of the regiment, much to the delight of its men. Again with his men, he was at the battle of Perryville on October 8, 1862, and the battle of Murfreesboro on December 31, 1862 and January 2, 1863. In both instances Quintard ministered to his men as a priest and a physician, working to the point of tears and exhaustion at Perryville.[6]

In early March, 1863, Quintard's role again changed. At the instance of the various chaplains of Polk's Corps, Quintard was assigned to duty at the corps hospitals, in order to minister to the needs of the sick and wounded there. During this interval he likely began his work on *The Confederate Soldier's Pocket Manual of Devotions*, which was published in 1863 through the financial assistance of J. K. Sass of Charleston, treasurer of the General Council of the Protestant Episcopal Church in the Confederate States. After a tour of the hospitals, Quintard returned to the army and resumed his ministry among the soldiers. Hearing that Bishop Stephen Elliott of Georgia was to visit the army, Quintard stepped up his efforts with the men and summoned the courage to confront the imposing army commander, Gen. Braxton Bragg, about his religious situation. The tearful Bragg asked that Quintard instruct him for confirmation in the

---

[6]Ibid., 46-61.

church, and was baptized and confirmed by Elliott in early June.[7]

Quintard remained with the Army of Tennessee through its defeat in the Tullahoma Campaign in late June and early July, 1863, and resumed his double duty as a surgeon treating the wounded in the days after the sanguinary Battle of Chickamauga. Quintard continued his service on the corps level, serving with his friend Leonidas Polk until the bishop was relieved as a result of a dispute with Bragg and transferred to a command in Mississippi. Quintard appears to have remained on duty with the Army of Tennessee until the Confederate defeat at Missionary Ridge occasioned a retreat to Dalton, Georgia. Bragg's resignation after the defeat cleared the way for Quintard to rejoin Polk. In early February, 1864, however, the new commander of the Army of Tennessee, Joseph E. Johnston, appointed Quintard chaplain at large with a base of operations in Atlanta, Georgia. [8]

With his customary energy, Quintard went to work, attending the army's hospitals and starting a small parish in Atlanta, St. Luke's. On April 22, 1864, Quintard assisted Bishop Elliott in a service of consecration of a church building erected in the space of six weeks. It was during this time that he likely compiled *Balm for the*

---

[7]Ibid., 62-72, 85.
[8]Ibid., 76-84.

Weary and the Wounded. Like *The Confederate Soldier's Pocket Manual of Devotions, Balm for the Weary and the Wounded* was published with the financial assistance of Mr. Sass. By the time Quintard received the first copies of *Balm for the Weary and the Wounded,* the Atlanta Campaign had begun, and Polk returned to the Army of Tennessee with reinforcements from his command in Mississippi. In the first days of June, Quintard sent his first four copies of *Balm for the Weary and the Wounded* to Polk, who studied them and then wrote inscriptions to each of Gen. Joseph E. Johnston, Lt. Gen. William J. Hardee, and Lt. Gen. John B. Hood, dated June 12, 1864. Copies were also sent to Bragg who was then at Richmond, and to Mary Lee, wife of Robert E. Lee, and were distributed to the hospitals. Confederate nurse Kate Cumming noted in her diary for June 10, 1864 that she had received a package of the books from Quintard, which one of the wounded soldiers in her charge seemed "to prize like gold."[9]

Polk never got to distribute the books to his friends. They were on his person when he was killed by a Federal shell on June 14, and were stained by the Bishop's blood, and were later sent to the intended recipients by members

---

[9]Ibid., 83-86; Kate Cumming, *A Journal of Hospital Life in the Confederate Army of Tennessee: From the Battle of Shiloh to the End of the War: with Sketches of Life and Character, and Brief Notices of Current Events During that Period,* (Louisville: John P. Morgan & Co., 1866) 132.

of Polk's staff with the bloodstains still on them. "Shocked and overwhelmed," Quintard participated in the funeral ceremonies for his friend at the new St. Luke's Church, and then accompanied the body to Augusta for burial. During the summer of 1864, Quintard continued his work with the army and, at the request of Bishop Stephen Elliott of Georgia, served a parish in Macon. Because of his failure to arrest Sherman's advance to Atlanta, Johnston was relieved and Hood appointed in his place. Quintard soon became a confidant of the general, and presented him for confirmation to Bishop Henry C. Lay of Arkansas in early August. When the city fell to the Federals in early September, 1864, Quintard escaped the city and joined his family in Columbus, Georgia. [10]

Beaten at Atlanta, within two months the Army of Tennessee was gamely advancing into Middle Tennessee, and with great joy, Quintard joined his army friends as they advanced into the well-familiar area south of Nashville. After the Army of Tennessee's terrible losses at the Battle of Franklin on November 30, 1864, Quintard prayerfully consoled the wounded, and sorrowfully buried the dead. A few days later, the faint spark of hope that

---

[10] William Mecklenburg Polk, *Leonidas Polk: Bishop and General* (New York: Longmans, Green & Co., 1915) 2:369-70, 387-88; Quintard, *Doctor Quintard*, 86-88; "Isham G. Harris as Warrior and Fugitive," *Atlanta Constitution*, August 1, 1897.

flared with the army's return to Middle Tennessee was brutally extinguished on the hills just south of Nashville on December 15 and 16, 1864, and Quintard joined the retreat, thinking of lost friends with a "bitter spirit."[11]

Journeying across the tottering Confederacy, Quintard spent the first few weeks of 1865 making his way home. Arriving back in Columbus in late February, Quintard attended to pastoral duties while he absorbed the news of the final struggle of the Army of Tennessee in North Carolina and the fall of Richmond. He was in the path of a heavily armed column of Federal cavalry that marched through Columbus on Easter Sunday, April 16, 1865, a week after the surrender at Appomattox. In the course of the invasion, Quintard and his neighbors were subjected to threats and thievery from members of the blue host. Accustomed to dealing with the highest ranking officers of the Confederate army, he obtained a personal interview with the Federal commander, Maj. Gen. James H. Wilson and secured guards for his home and that of a neighbor.[12]

With the war's end, there was need for reconciliation between the two warring sections. Quintard arrived in Nashville and soon found himself ministering to members of the Federal garrison, to the point that he felt that he had "been unconsciously converted from a

---

[11]Quintard, *Doctor Quintard*, 81-109, 203.
[12]Ibid., 253-57.

Confederate to a Federal Chaplain", much to the appreciation of the officers of the Federal occupation force. As Bishop Otey died during the war, the Episcopalian clergy of Tennessee met to elect a new bishop, and Quintard was chosen. The General Convention of the Protestant Episcopal Church in the United States of America met in Philadelphia in early October, 1865, rejoining the southern and northern branches of the church. Quintard was consecrated as Bishop of Tennessee, and at that point "felt that the war between the states was indeed over."[13]

Having been a significant part of the beginning of the reconciliation of the northern and southern branches of the Episcopal Church, Bishop Quintard set out to restore the work of the church that was disrupted by the war. Within the Diocese of Tennessee, only three church buildings were undamaged. Of those that survived with damage, few were useable, and their congregations scattered. Quintard vigorously went to work. In his first full year of his Episcopate, he confirmed 470 people, preached 152 sermons, and gave 112 addresses. His efforts continued for over thirty years, and the number of parishes and missions of the Diocese doubled during that

---

[13]Ibid., 127-29; *Journal of the Proceedings of the Bishops, Clergy and Laity of the Protestant Episcopal Church in the United States of America Assembled in a General Convention* (Boston: William A. Hall, 1865), 165.

time. In the estimation of one historian, Quintard was "probably the most influential Episcopalian in the South during Reconstruction."[14]

Quintard's second great work of reconstruction was to take up the mantle of his friends Otey and Polk in the cause of the University of the South. In 1856, Polk proposed establishing an institution of higher education to his nine fellow southern bishops. With Otey and Bishop Elliott of Georgia, the future Confederate general became a driving force in the organization of the university. In October, 1860, then-Rev. Quintard joined Polk, Otey, Elliott and five other southern bishops at a ceremony to lay a cornerstone on the Cumberland Plateau at Sewanee, Tennessee. The new university sat upon an almost 10,000 acre domain, 5,000 of which were donated by the Sewanee Mining Company upon the condition that if the school was not operating within ten years, the gift would revert. Unfortunately, before the new institution could take root, the Civil War intervened. Polk's last visit to Sewanee occurred when the Army of Tennessee retreated across the domain in July, 1863. In

---

[14]Quintard, *Doctor Quintard*, 131-38; Arthur Ben Chitty, *Reconstruction at Sewanee: The Founding of the University of the South and its First Administration, 1857-1872*, 1954, reprint (Sewanee, Tennessee: Proctor's Hall Press, 1993), 89-91; "Death of the Bishop," *Memphis Commercial Appeal*, February 16, 1898.

the course of the war what few frame buildings which existed on the site were burned, the cornerstone laid in 1860 was blown to pieces, and the financial pledges made by the once prosperous southern elite were rendered effectively worthless.[15]

But Polk's dream did not die with him at Pine Mountain. In September, 1865, Quintard, Tennessee clergyman Rev. David Pise and university trustee George Fairbanks of Florida met on a train in Middle Tennessee and resolved to revive the University of the South. Quintard obtained the necessary authorization from the university trustees, built a residence at Sewanee, and devoted much of his considerable energies in the next few years to getting the institution in operation, timely averting the reversion of the 5,000 acres to the Sewanee Mining Company. Quintard became the university's primary fundraiser and first vice-chancellor, and traveled extensively within the United States and England to solicit funds for the institution. While Quintard's efforts were not the sole reason for the university's survival, without his "courageous faith and invincible zeal" it likely would not exist today.[16]

Quintard died on February 15, 1898, the same day that the battleship *Maine* exploded in Havana Harbor.

---

[15]Chitty, *Reconstruction at Sewanee*, 45-50, 59-66, 83.

[16]Ibid., 89-91, 101-8, 172, 174; Quintard, *Doctor Quintard*, 140-150; "Death of the Bishop".

Although Quintard's ministry was long and varied, it was his special call to minister to young men that first brought him into the Confederate army as a chaplain in 1861 and it was that call that led him tirelessly to work for the reestablishment and funding of the University of the South. It was the doubtless the same zeal for that calling that led Quintard to compose *The Confederate Soldier's Pocket Manual of Devotions* and *Balm for the Weary and the Wounded.* While he could not possibly personally attend to every Confederate soldier, these two books were his effort to reach beyond that practical physical limitation to provide encouragement, comfort and consolation to the whole army. These simple volumes shine through to us almost 150 years later as tangible evidence of a man's love for the unique flock of young men he was called to serve.

—Sam Davis Elliott

THE CONFEDERATE

SOLDIER'S POCKET

MANUAL OF DEVOTIONS.

THE DUTIES OF A CHRISTIAN.

That man leads a sincere Christian life,

1st. Who endeavors to serve and obey God to the best of his understanding and power.

2dly. Who strives to please his neighbor to edification.

3dly. Who endeavors to do his duty in that state of life unto which it has pleased God to call him.

Whoever would continue in the practice of these things unto his life's end, it is necessary that he should call himself often to an account whether he does so or not; constantly pray for grace to know, and to do his duty; and preserve himself in such a teachable temper as to be always ready to receive the truth when it is fairly proposed to him.

PRAYER, AND HOPE OF VICTORY.

Now may the God of grace and power
Attend his people's humble cry;
Defend them in the needful hour,
And send deliverance from on high.

In His salvation is our hope;
And in the name of Israel's God
Our troops shall lift their banners up,
Our navies spread their flags abroad.

Some trust in horses trained for war,
And some of chariots make their boast;
Our surest expectations are
From Thee, the Lord of heavenly hosts.

Then save us, Lord, from slavish fear,
And let our trust be firm and strong,
Till Thy salvation shall appear,
And hymns of peace conclude our song.

A bruised reed shall He not break, and smoking flax shall
He not quench;
St. Matt. xii, 20.

STRENGTH IN THE WEAK.

Will Jesus accept such a heart as mine—this erring,
treacherous, traitor heart? The past! how many for-gotten
vows—broken covenants—prayerless days! How often
have I made new resolutions, and as often has the reed
succumbed to the first blast of temptation, and the
burning flax been well nigh quenched by guilty omissions
and guiltier commissions! Oh, my soul! thou art low
indeed—the things that remain seem "ready to die." But
thy Saviour-God will not give thee "over unto death."
The reed is bruised; but He will not pluck it up by the
roots. The flax is reduced to a smoking ember; but He
will fan the decaying flame. Why wound thy loving
Saviour's heart by these repeated declensions? He will
not—can not give thee up. Go, mourn thy weakness and
unbelief. Cry unto the strong for strength. Weary and
faint one! thou hast an omnipotent arm to lean on. "He
fainteth not, neither is weary!" Listen to his own gracious
assurance: "Fear not, for I am with thee. Be not dismayed,
for I am thy God. I will strengthen thee; yea, I will help
thee with the right hand of my righteousness!" Leaving all
thy false props and refuges, be this thy resolve: "In the
Lord put I my trust: why say ye to my soul, flee as a bird to
your mountain?"

All things work together for good to
them that love God.
Rom. viii, 28.

PROVIDENTIAL OVERRULING.

My soul, be still! thou art in the hands of thy covenant
God. Were these strange vicissitudes in thy history the
result of accident, or chance, thou mightest well be
overwhelmed; but "all things," and this thing (be what it
may) which may be now disquieting thee is one of these
"all things," that are so working mysteriously for thy good.

TRUST THY GOD.

He will not deceive thee—thy interests are with Him in safe custody. When sight says "all these things are against me," let faith rebuke the hasty conclusion, and say "shall not the Judge of all the earth do right?" How often does God hedge up our way with thorns, to elicit simple trust! How seldom can we see all things so working for our good! But it is better discipline to believe it. Oh, for faith amid frowning providences to say "I know that Thy judgments are good;" and, relying in the dark, to exclaim "Though He slay me, yet will I trust Him!" Blessed Jesus! to Thee are committed the reins of this universal empire. The same hand that was once nailed to the cross is now wielding the sceptre on the throne—" all power given unto Thee in heaven and in earth."

How can I doubt the wisdom, and faithfulness, and love of the most mysterious earthly dealing, when I know that the roll of providence is thus in the hands of Him who has given the mightiest pledge omnipotence could give of His tender interest in my soul's well-being by giving Himself for me?

All the paths of the Lord are mercy and truth unto such as
keep His covenant and His testimonies.

Ps. xxv, 10.

SAFE WALKING.

The paths of the Lord? My soul! never follow thine own
paths. If thou dost so, thou wilt be in danger often of
following sight rather than faith—choosing the evil, and
refusing the good. But "commit thy way unto the Lord,
and He shall bring it to pass." Let this be thy prayer:
"Show me Thy ways, O Lord: teach me Thy paths." Oh!
for Caleb's spirit, "wholly to follow the Lord my God"—
to follow Him when self must be sacrificed, and hardship
must be borne, and trials await me. To "walk with
God"—to ask in simple faith, "What wouldst thou have
me to do?" to have no will of my own, save this, that
God's will is to be my will. Here is safety— here is
happiness. Fearlessly follow the guiding Pillar. He will lead
you by a right way, though it may be by a way of
hardship, and crosses, and losses, and privations, to the
city of habitation. Oh! the blessedness of thus lying
passive in the hands of God; saying, "Undertake Thou for
me!"—dwelling with holy gratitude on past mercies and
interpositions—taking these as pledges of future
faithfulness and love—hearing His voice behind us amid
life's manifold perplexities, exclaiming, "This is the way,
walk ye in it!"

Happy, O my soul! will it be for thee, if thou canst form the resolve in a strength greater than thine own: "This God shall be my God for ever and ever; He shall be my guide even unto death."

THE COMFORTABLE WORDS.

Hear what comfortable words our Saviour Christ saith unto all who truly turn to Him:

"Come unto me, all ye that travail and are
heavy laden, and I will refresh you."
—St. Matt. xi, 28.

"So God loved the world, that He gave His only begotten
son, to the end that all that believed in Him should not
perish, but have everlasting life."
—St. John iii, 16.

Hear, also, what St. Paul saith:

"This is a true saying, and worthy of all men to be
received, that Christ Jesus came into the world to save
sinners."
—1 Tim. i, 15.

Hear, also, what St. John saith:

"If any man sin, we have an advocate with the Father,
Jesus Christ the righteous; and He is the propitiation for
our sins."
—1 John ii, 1, 2.

LOOK UNTO JESUS.

He was despised and rejected of men; His life was sought for by Herod; He was tempted by Satan; hated by that world He came to save; set at naught by His own people; called a deceiver and a dealer with the devil; was driven from place to place, and had not where to lay His head; betrayed by one disciple, and forsaken by all the rest; falsely accused, spit upon, scourged; set at naught by Herod and his men of war; given up by Pilate to the will of His enemies; had a murderer preferred before Him; was condemned to a most cruel and shameful death; crucified between two thieves; reviled in the midst of His torments; had gall and vinegar given Him to drink; suffered a most bitter death, submitting with patience to the will of His Father.

O Jesu, who now sittest at the right hand of God, to succor all who suffer in a righteous way; be thou my advocate for grace, that in all my sufferings I may follow thy example, and run with patience the race that is set before me.
—AMEN.

CHRIST OUR REFUGE.

Jesus, Saviour of my soul,
Let me to Thy bosom fly,
While the waves of trouble roll,
While the tempest still is high:
Hide me, O my Saviour, hide,
Till the storm of life is past;
Safe into the haven guide;
O receive my soul at last.

Other refuge have I none,
Hangs my helpless soul on Thee,
Leave, ah, leave me not alone;
Still support and comfort me:
All my trust on Thee is stayed,
All my hope from Thee I bring;
Cover my defenceless head
With the shadow of Thy wing.

AN ACT OF FAITH.

I believe in God, the Father Almighty, maker of heaven and earth:

And in Jesus Christ, His only son, our Lord; who was conceived by the Holy Ghost; born of the Virgin Mary; suffered under Pontius Pilate, was crucified, dead, and buried; He descended into hell; the third day He rose from the dead; He ascended into heaven, and sitteth on the right hand of God, the Father Almighty; from thence he shall come to judge the quick and the dead.

I believe in the Holy Ghost; the holy Catholic Church; the communion of saints; the forgiveness of sins; the resurrection of the body, and the life everlasting.
AMEN.
Prayer.

Almighty God, whom without faith it is not possible to please, enable me, I beseech Thee, so perfectly to believe in Thy son Jesus Christ that my faith in Thy sight may never be reproved; and grant that, as I am called to a knowledge of Thy grace and faith in Thee,

I may avoid all those things that are contrary to my profession, and follow all such as are agreeable to the same; through Jesus Christ our Lord.
AMEN.

THE TEN COMMANDMENTS.

"If ye keep my commandments ye shall abide in my love;
even as I have kept my Father's commandments, and
abide in His love."
—St. John xv, 10.

God spake these words and said:

I. Thou shalt have none other gods but me.

II. Thou shalt not make to thyself any graven image, nor
the likeness of anything that is in heaven above, or in the
earth beneath, or in the waters under the earth. Thou
shalt not bow down to them nor worship them: for I the
Lord thy God am a jealous God, and visit the sins of the
fathers upon the children, unto the third and fourth
generation of them that hate me; and show mercy unto
thousands of them that love me, and keep my
commandments.

III. Thou shalt not take the name of the Lord thy God in
vain: for the Lord will not hold him guiltless that taketh
His name in vain.

IV. Remember that thou keep holy the Sabbath-day. Six
days shalt thou labor, and do all that thou hast to do: but
the seventh day is the Sabbath of the Lord thy God. In it
thou shalt do no manner of work; thou, and thy son and

thy daughter, thy man servant, and thy maid servant, thy cattle, and the stranger that is within thy gates. For in six days the Lord made heaven and earth, the sea, and all that in them is, and rested the seventh day: wherefore the Lord blessed the seventh day, and hallowed it.

V. Honor thy father and thy mother; that thy days may be long in the land which the Lord thy God giveth thee.

VI. Thou shalt do no murder.

VII. Thou shalt not commit adultery.

VIII. Thou shalt not steal.

IX. Thou shalt not bear false witness against thy neighbor.

X. Thou shalt not covet thy neighbor's house, thou shalt not covet thy neighbor's wife, nor his servant, nor his maid, nor his ox, nor his ass, nor anything that is his.

Lord have mercy upon me, and write all these Thy laws in my heart, I beseech Thee. AMEN.

Hear also what our Lord Jesus Christ saith:

Thou shalt love the Lord thy God with all thy heart, and with all thy soul, and with all thy mind. This is the first and great commandment. And the second is like unto it: thou shalt love thy neighbor as thyself. On these two commandments hang all the law and the prophets.

O Almighty Lord and everlasting God, vouchsafe, I beseech Thee, to direct, sanctify, and govern both my heart and body, in the ways of Thy laws, and in the works of Thy commandments; that through Thy most mighty protection, both here and ever, I may be preserved in body and soul; through our Lord and Saviour Jesus Christ. AMEN.

MORNING PRAYER.

I will lift up mine eyes unto the hills, from whence cometh my help.

My help cometh even from the Lord, who hath made heaven and earth.

He will not suffer thy foot to be moved; and He that keepeth thee will not sleep.

Behold, He that keepeth Israel shall neither slumber nor sleep.

The Lord himself is thy keeper; the Lord is thy defence upon thy right hand;

So that the sun shall not burn thee by day, neither the moon by night.

The Lord shall preserve thee from all evil; yea, it is even He that shall keep thy soul.

The Lord shall preserve thy going out, and thy coming in, from this time forth for evermore.

O God, who art the author of peace and lover of concord, in knowledge of whom standeth our eternal life, whose service is perfect freedom; defend me Thy humble servant in all assaults of my enemies; that I, surely trusting in Thy defence, may not fear the Power of any adversaries, through the might of Jesus Christ our Lord. AMEN.

O Lord our heavenly Father, almighty and everlasting God, who hast safely brought me to the beginning of this day; defend me in the same with Thy mighty power: and grant that this day I fall into no sin, neither run into any kind of danger; but that all my doings, being ordered by Thy governance, may be righteous in Thy sight; through Jesus Christ our Lord. AMEN.

O most mighty God, and merciful Father, who hast compassion upon all men, and hatest nothing that Thou hast made; who wouldst not the death of a sinner, but rather that he should turn from his sin, and be saved; mercifully forgive me my trespasses; receive and comfort me, who am grieved and wearied with the burden of my sins. Thy property is always ways to have mercy; to Thee only it appertaineth to forgive sins. Spare me, therefore, good Lord, spare Thy servant whom Thou hast redeemed; enter not into judgment with Thy servant who is vile earth and a miserable sinner; but so turn Thine anger from me, who meekly acknowledge my vileness, and truly repent me of my faults, and so make haste to help me in this world, that I may ever live with

Thee in the world to come, through Jesus Christ our Lord. AMEN.

Our Father, who art in heaven, hallowed be Thy name. Thy kingdom come. Thy will be done on earth, as it is in heaven. Give us this day our daily bread. And forgive us our trespasses, as we forgive those who trespass against us. And lead us not into temptation; but deliver us from evil: for Thine is the kingdom, and the power, and the glory, for ever and ever. AMEN.

The grace of our Lord Jesus Christ, and the love of God, and the fellowship of the Holy Ghost be with us all evermore. AMEN.

EVENING PRAYER.

Psalm cxli.

Lord, I call upon Thee; haste Thee unto me, and consider my voice, when I cry unto Thee.

Let my prayer be set forth in Thy sight as the incense; and let the lifting up of my hands be an evening sacrifice.

Set a watch, O Lord, before my mouth, and keep the door of my lips.

O let not my heart be inclined to any evil thing; let me not be occupied in ungodly works with the men that work wickedness lest I eat of such things as please them.

Keep me from the snare that they have laid for me, and from the traps of the wicked doers.

Let the ungodly fall into their own nets together, and let me ever escape them.

O God, from whom all holy desires, all good counsels, and all just works do proceed, give unto thy servant that peace which the world can not give, that my heart may be set to obey thy commandments; and also, that by thee I, being defended from the fear of my enemies, may pass my time in rest and quietness; through the merits of Jesus Christ our Saviour. AMEN.

O Lord, our heavenly Father, by whose almighty power I have been preserved this day; by thy great mercy defend me, and all who are dear to me, from all perils and dangers of this night; for the love of thy only Son our Saviour Jesus Christ. AMEN.

Almighty and everlasting God, who hatest nothing that Thou hast made, and dost forgive the sins of all those who are penitent; create and make in me a new and contrite heart, that I, worthily lamenting my sins, and acknowledging my wretchedness, may obtain of Thee, the God of all mercy, perfect remission and forgiveness; through Jesus Christ our Lord. AMEN.

O everlasting God, who hast ordained and constituted the services of angels and men in a wonderful order; mercifully grant, that as Thy holy angels always do Thee service in heaven, so, by Thy appointment, they may succor and defend me on earth; through Jesus Christ our Lord. AMEN.

Our Father, who art in heaven, hallowed be Thy name. Thy kingdom come. Thy will be done on earth, as it is in heaven. Give us this day our daily bread. And forgive us our trespasses, as we forgive those who trespass against us. And lead us not into temptation; but deliver us from evil: for Thine is the kingdom, and the power, and the glory, for ever and ever. AMEN.

Unto God's gracious mercy and protection I commit my soul and body. The Lord bless me and keep me. The Lord make his face to shine upon me, and be gracious unto me. The Lord lift up His countenance upon me, and give me peace, both now and evermore. AMEN.

THE LITANY.

(To be used on Wednesdays, Fridays, and Sundays.)

O God the Father of heaven, have mercy upon me; keep and defend me.

O God the Son, Redeemer of the world, have mercy upon me; save and deliver me.

O God the Holy Ghost, have mercy upon me; strengthen and comfort me.

Remember not, Lord, mine offences, nor the offences of my forefathers; neither take Thou vengeance of our sins. Spare us, good Lord, spare Thy people, whom Thou hast redeemed with Thy most precious blood, and be not angry with us for ever.

From Thy wrath and heavy indignation; from the guilt and burden of my sins; from the dreadful sentence of the last Judgment, good Lord deliver me.

From the sting and terrors of conscience; from impatience, distrust, or despair; from extremity of sickness and pain, which may withdraw my mind from God, good Lord deliver me.

From the bitter pangs of eternal death; from the gates of hell; from the powers of darkness, and from the illusions of Satan, good Lord deliver me.

By Thy manifold and great mercies; by Thy manifold and great merits; by Thine agony and bloody sweat; by Thy bitter cross and passion; by Thy mighty resurrection; by Thy glorious ascension, and most acceptable intercession; and by the graces of the Holy Ghost, good Lord deliver me.

For the glory of Thy name; for Thy loving mercy and truth's sake, good Lord deliver me.

In my last and greatest need; in the hour of death, and in the day of Judgment, good Lord deliver me.

O Lamb of God, who takest away the sins of the world, grant me Thy peace.

O Lamb of God, who takest away the sins of the world, have mercy upon me.

O God, merciful Father, who despisest not the sighing of a contrite heart, nor the desire of such as are sorrowful, mercifully assist my prayers which I make before Thee in all my troubles and adversities, whensoever they oppress me; and graciously hear me, that those evils which the craft and subtlety of the devil or man worketh against me may, by Thy good providence, be brought to naught; that

I, Thy servant, being hurt by no persecutions, may evermore give thanks unto Thee in Thy holy Church; through Jesus Christ our Lord. AMEN.

The grace of our Lord Jesus Christ, etc. AMEN.

Prayers that may be added to the morning and evening devotions.

Almighty God, Father of our Lord Jesus Christ, maker of all things, judge of all men. I acknowledge and bewail my manifold sins and wickedness, which I, from time to time, most grievously have committed, by thought, word, and deed, against Thy divine majesty, provoking most justly Thy wrath and indignation against me. I do earnestly repent, and am heartily sorry for these my misdoings; the remembrance of them is grievous unto me; the burden of them is intolerable. Have mercy upon me, have mercy upon me, most merciful Father; for Thy son our Lord Jesus Christ's sake, forgive me all that is past; and grant that I may ever hereafter serve and please Thee in newness of life, to the honor and glory of Thy name; through Jesus Christ our Lord. AMEN.

O God, Holy Ghost, sanctifier of the faithful, visit me, I pray Thee, with Thy love and favor; enlighten my mind more and more with the light of the everlasting gospel; graft in my heart a love of the truth; increase in me true religion; nourish me with all goodness; and of Thy great mercy keep me in the same, O blessed Spirit, whom, with the Father and the Son together, we worship and glorify as one God, world without end. AMEN.

O Almighty God, who hast knit together thine elect in one communion and fellowship, in the mystical body of Thy Son Christ our Lord, grant me grace so to follow Thy blessed saints in all virtuous and godly living that we may come to those unspeakable joys which Thou hast prepared for those who unfeignedly love Thee; through Jesus Christ our Lord. AMEN.

O God, the protector of all that trust in Thee, without whom nothing is strong, nothing is holy, increase and multiply upon me Thy mercy, that, Thou being my ruler and guide, I may so pass through things temporal that I finally lose not the things eternal. Grant this, O heavenly Father, for Jesus Christ's sake, our Lord. AMEN.

Almighty and everlasting God, who, of Thy tender love toward mankind, hast sent Thy Son, our Saviour Jesus Christ, to take upon Him our flesh, and to suffer death upon the cross, that all mankind should follow the example of His great humility, mercifully grant that I may both follow the example of His patience and be made a partaker of His resurrection; through the same Jesus Christ our Lord. AMEN.

Almighty God, who through Thine only begotten Son Jesus Christ has overcome death, and opened unto us the gate of everlasting life, I humbly beseech Thee that as, by Thy special grace preventing me, Thou dost put into my mind good desires, so by Thy continual help I may bring the same to good effect; through Jesus Christ our Lord, who liveth and reigneth with Thee and the Holy Ghost, ever one God, world without end. AMEN.

O Almighty God, the supreme governor of all things, whose power no creature is able to resist, to whom it belongeth justly to punish sinners, and to be merciful to those who truly repent, save and deliver me, I humbly beseech Thee, from the hands of my enemies; abate their pride, assuage their malice, and confound their devices; that I, being armed with Thy defence, may be preserved evermore from all perils to glorify Thee, who art the only giver of all victory through the merits of Thy Son Jesus Christ our Lord. AMEN.

O most powerful and glorious Lord God, the Lord of hosts, that rulest and commandest all things: Thou sittest in the throne judging right, and therefore we make our address to Thy Divine Majesty, in our necessity, that Thou wouldest take the cause into Thine own hand, and judge between us and our enemies. Stir up Thy strength, O Lord, and come and help us; for Thou givest not always the battle to the strong, but canst save by many or by few. O let not our sins cry against us for vengeance; but hear us, Thy poor servants, begging mercy, and imploring

Thy help, and that Thou wouldest be a defence unto us against the face of the enemy. Make it appear that Thou art our Saviour and mighty Deliverer; through Jesus Christ our Lord. AMEN.

O Lord, our heavenly Father, the high and mighty Ruler of the universe, who dost from Thy throne behold all the dwellers upon earth: most heartily I beseech Thee to behold and bless Thy servant, the President of the Confederate States, and all others in authority; and so replenish them with the grace of Thy Holy Spirit, that they may always incline to Thy will, and walk in Thy way. Endue them plenteously with heavenly gifts; grant them in health and prosperity long to live; and finally, after this life, to attain everlasting joy and felicity; through Jesus Christ our Lord. AMEN.

COLLECTS FOR SEVERAL GRACES.

For Faith.

O blessed Lord, whom without faith it is impossible to please, let Thy Spirit, I beseech Thee, work in me such a faith as may be acceptable in Thy sight, even such as may show itself by my works, that it may enable me to overcome the world, and conform me to the image of that Christ on whom I believe; that so at the last I may receive the end of my faith, even the salvation of my soul, by the same Jesus Christ our Lord. AMEN.

For Hope.

O Lord, who art the hope of all the ends of the earth, let me never be destitute of a well-grounded hope, nor yet possessed with a vain presumption; suffer me not to think Thou wilt either be reconciled to my sins or reject my repentance; but give me, I beseech Thee, such hope as may both encourage and enable me to purify myself, even as Thou art pure, that when Thou shalt appear, I may be made like unto Thee, in thy eternal and glorious kingdom, where, with the Father and the Holy Ghost, Thou livest and reignest one God, world without end. AMEN.

For the Love of God.
O God, who hast prepared for those who love Thee such good things as pass man's understanding, pour into our hearts such love toward Thee that we, loving Thee above all things, may obtain Thy promises, which exceed all that we can desire; through Jesus Christ our Lord. AMEN.

For Charity.
O Lord, who hast taught us that all our doings without charity are nothing worth, send Thy Holy Ghost, and pour into our hearts that most excellent gift of charity, the very bond of peace and of all virtues, without which whosoever liveth is counted dead before Thee, Grant this for Thine only Son Jesus Christ's sake. AMEN.

For Chastity.
O holy and immaculate Jesus, who wast conceived in a virgin's womb, and who dost still love to dwell in pure and virgin hearts; give me, I beseech Thee, the grace to keep my heart with all diligence, and to withstand all temptations of the flesh, and with pure and clean heart to follow Thee, the only God, even for Thine own merits' and mercies' sake. AMEN.

For Contentedness.
O God, Heavenly Father, who by Thy Son Jesus Christ hast promised to all them that seek Thy kingdom and its righteousness all things necessary to their bodily sustenance, let me always fully resign myself to Thy disposal, having no desires of my own, and teach me in

whatsoever state I am therewith to be content. Grant me grace to forsake all covetous desires, and inordinate love of riches, and so to pass through things temporal that I finally lose not the things eternal; through Jesus Christ our Lord. AMEN.

For Contrition.

Almighty and everlasting God, who hatest nothing that Thou hast made, and dost forgive the sins of all those who are penitent, create and make in us new and contrite hearts, that we, worthily lamenting our sins, and acknowledging our wretchedness, may obtain of Thee, the God of all mercy, perfect remission and forgiveness; through Jesus Christ our Lord. AMEN.

For Devotion.

Most gracious Lord God, who hast not only permitted, but invited us miserable and needy creatures to present our petitions to Thee; grant that I may set a true value on this most valuable privilege, and take delight in approaching Thee. Give me a hearty desire to pray, and such fixedness and attention of mind as no wandering thoughts may interrupt, that I may no more incur the guilt of drawing near to Thee with my lips when my heart is far from Thee, or have my prayers turned into sin; but may so ask, that I may receive; seek, that I may find; knock, that it may be opened unto me; that from praying to Thee here I may be translated to the praising Thee eternally in Thy glory; through the merits and intercession of Jesus Christ our Lord. AMEN.

For Diligence.

O God, who hast commanded that no man should be idle, but that we should all work with our hands the thing that is good, grant that I may diligently do my duty in that station of life to which Thou hast been pleased to call me. Give me a grace that I may improve all the talents Thou hast committed to my trust; and that no worldly business, no worldly pleasures may ever divert me from the thoughts of the life to come; through Jesus Christ our Lord. AMEN.

For the Fear of God.

O most glorious God, who only art high and to be feared, put Thy fear into my heart that I may not sin against Thee, nor sacrilegiously profane any holy thing. O let me never so misplace my fear as to be afraid of man, whose breath is in his nostrils; but fill me, O Lord, with the Spirit of thy holy fear, which is the beginning of wisdom, and keep me in a constant conformity to Thy holy will, that I may, with fear and trembling, work out my own salvation, through Jesus Christ our Lord. AMEN.

For Humility.

Almighty God, who resisteth the proud and giveth grace to the humble, mercifully grant that I may follow the example of the great humility of Thy blessed Son, who did humble Himself to take upon Him our flesh, and to suffer death upon the cross: convince me that I am less than the least of all Thy mercies; that as I am vile in myself, so let me be vile in mine own eyes, and may therefore esteem every man better than myself. Grant this, O Father, for Thy Son Jesus Christ's sake. AMEN.

For Justice.
O Thou King of righteousness, who hast commanded us to keep judgment, and do justice, be pleased by Thy grace to cleanse my heart and hands from all fraud and injustice. Grant that I may most strictly observe that sacred rule of doing unto all men as I would they should do unto me; that I may hurt nobody by word or deed, but be true and just in all my dealings; that so, keeping innocency and taking heed unto the thing that is right, I may have peace at the last, even peace with Thee, through Jesus Christ our Lord. AMEN.

For Sincerity.
O holy Lord, who searchest the heart and triest the reins; try me, I beseech Thee, and seek the ground of my heart; purge it from all hypocrisy and insincerity, and suffer not any accursed thing to lurk within me; give me truth in the inward parts, and purity of heart, that I may be prepared to see Thee in Thy kingdom, through Jesus Christ our Lord. AMEN.

For Temperance.
Gracious Lord, who hast afforded us the use of Thy good creatures for the refreshment of our bodies, and art the Author and Giver of all good things, give me grace always to use this liberty with thankfulness and moderation, that

my table may never be made a snare unto me. And grant that my pursuits may not be after the meat that perisheth, but after that which endureth unto everlasting life; that, hungering and thirsting after righteousness, I may be filled with Thy grace here, and Thy glory hereafter, through Jesus Christ our Lord. AMEN.

For Thankfulness.

Most gracious and bountiful Lord, who fillest all things living with good, and hast taught us that it is a joyful and pleasant thing to be thankful, suffer me not, I beseech Thee, to lose my part in that divine pleasure, but grant that as I daily receive blessings from Thee, so may I daily, from an affectionate and devout heart, offer up thanks to Thee; let Thy mercies lead me to repentance, and give me grace to improve them all to the advancement of Thy glory, and the furtherance of my salvation, through Jesus Christ our Lord. AMEN.

For Trust in God.

O God, who never failest to help and govern them whom Thou dost bring up in Thy steadfast fear and love, grant, I pray Thee, that I may lean only upon the hope of Thy heavenly grace, and in all my troubles put my whole trust and confidence in Thy mercy, casting all my care upon Thee, and being careful for nothing but to keep Thy testimonies, and think upon Thy commandments to do them. Grant this, O Father, for Jesus Christ's sake. AMEN.

For Perseverance.

O eternal God, who seest my weakness, and knowest the number and strength of the temptations against which I have to struggle, leave me not to myself, but cover Thou my head in the day of battle, and in all Spiritual combats make me more than conqueror through Him that loved me. O let no terrors or flatteries, either of the world or my own flesh, ever draw me from my obedience to Thee; but grant that I may continue steadfast, immovable, always abounding in the work of the Lord; and, by patient continuance in well doing, seek, and at last obtain glory, and honor, and immortality, and eternal life, through Jesus Christ our Lord. AMEN.

For the members of our family from whom we are separated.

O God, merciful and gracious, who art everywhere present, let thy loving mercy and compassion descend upon the heads of Thy servants, the members of my family from whom I am now separated; depute Thy holy angels to guard their persons, Thy holy spirit to guide their souls, Thy providence to minister to their necessities; let Thy blessing be upon them night and day; sanctify them in their bodies, souls, and spirits; keep them unblamable to the coming of the Lord Jesus, and make them and me to dwell with Thee for ever in the light of Thy countenance, and in Thy glory for Jesus' sake. AMEN.

A FORM OF THANKSGIVING
AFTER VICTORY.

Psalm.[1]

If the Lord had not been on our side, now may we say; if the Lord himself had not been on our side when men rose up against us;

They had swallowed us up quick, when they were so wrathfully displeased at us.

Yea, the waters had drowned us, and the stream had gone over our souls: the deep waters of the proud had gone over our souls.

But praised be the Lord, who hath not given us over as a prey unto them.

The Lord hath wrought a mighty salvation for us.

We got not this by our own sword, neither was it our own arm that saved us; but Thy right hand, and Thine arm, and the light of Thy countenance, because Thou hadst a favor unto us.

[1 *Psalm*, here, refers to a church psalm not a psalm from the bible.]

The Lord hath appeared for us; the Lord hath covered our heads, and made us to stand in the day of battle.

The Lord hath appeared for us; the Lord hath overthrown our enemies, and dashed in pieces those that rose up against us.

Therefore, not unto us, O Lord, not unto us; but unto Thy name be given the glory.

The Lord hath done great things for us; the Lord hath done great things for us whereof we rejoice.

Our help standeth in the name of the Lord, who hath made heaven and earth.

Blessed be the name of the Lord from this time forth for evermore.

Glory be to the Father, and to the Son, and to the Holy Ghost.

As it was in the beginning, is now, and ever shall be, world without end. AMEN.

TE DEUM LAUDAMUS.

We praise Thee, O God, we acknowledge Thee to be the Lord.

All the earth doth worship Thee, the Father everlasting.

To Thee all Angels cry aloud; the heavens and all the powers therein.

To Thee Cherubim and Seraphim continually do cry;

Holy, holy, holy, Lord God of Sabbaoth ; heaven and earth are full of the majesty of Thy glory.

The glorious company of the Apostles praise Thee.

The goodly fellowship of the Prophets praise Thee.

The noble army of Martyrs praise Thee.

The holy Church throughout all the world doth acknowledge Thee;

The Father of an infinite Majesty;

Thine adorable, true, and only Son;

Also, the Holy Ghost, the Comforter.

Thou art the King of glory, O Christ.

Thou art the everlasting Son of the Father.

When Thou tookest upon Thee to deliver man, Thou didst humble Thyself to be born of a virgin.

When Thou hadst overcome the sharpness of death, Thou didst open the kingdom of heaven to all believers.

Thou sittest at the right hand of God, in the glory of the Father.

We believe that Thou shalt come to be our Judge.

We therefore pray Thee to help Thy servants, whom Thou hast redeemed with Thy precious blood.

Make them to be numbered with Thy saints, in glory everlasting.

O Lord, save Thy people, and bless Thine heritage.

Govern them, and lift them up for ever.

Day by day we magnify Thee;

And we worship Thy name ever, world without end.

Vouchsafe, O Lord, to keep us this day without sin.

O Lord, have mercy upon us, have mercy upon us.

O Lord, let thy mercy be upon us, as our trust is in Thee.

O Lord, in Thee have I trusted; let me never be confounded.

COLLECT.

O Almighty God, the sovereign Commander of all the world, in whose hand is power and might, which none is able to withstand; I bless and magnify Thy great and glorious name for this happy victory, the whole glory whereof we do ascribe to Thee, who art the only giver of victory.

And I beseech Thee, give me grace to improve this great mercy to Thy glory, the advancement of Thy gospel, the honor of my country, and, as much as in me lieth, to the good of all mankind.

And I beseech Thee give us all such a sense of this great mercy, as may engage us to a true thankfulness, such as may appear in our lives by an humble, obedient, and holy walking before Thee all our days, through Jesus Christ our Lord, to whom, with Thee and the Holy Spirit, as for all Thy mercies, so in particular for this victory and deliverance be all glory and honor, world without end. AMEN.

HYMNS.

I.
C. M.
Scriptures.

Father of mercies! in Thy word
What endless glory shines!
For ever be Thy name adored
For these celestial lines.

Here may the wretched sons of want
Exhaustless riches find;
Riches above what earth can grant,
And lasting as the mind.

Here the fair tree of knowledge grows,
And yields a free repast;
Sublimer sweets than nature knows
Invite the longing taste.

Here the Redeemer's welcome voice
Spreads heavenly peace around,
And life and everlasting joys
Attend the blissful sound.

O may these heavenly pages be
My ever dear delight,
And still new beauties may I see,

And still increasing light.

Divine Instructor! gracious Lord,
Be Thou for ever near;
Teach me to love Thy sacred word,
And view my Saviour there.

II.
The Christian Life.

Nearer, my God, to Thee!
Nearer to Thee!
E'en though it be a cross
That raiseth me;
Still all my song shall be,
Nearer, my God, to Thee,
Nearer to Thee.

Though like a wanderer,
Weary and lone,
Darkness comes over me,
My rest a stone;
Yet in my dreams I'd be
Nearer, my God, to Thee,
Nearer to Thee!

There let my way appear
Steps unto heaven;
All that Thou sendest me
In mercy given;
Angels to beckon me
Nearer, my God, to Thee,
Nearer to Thee!

Then with my waking thoughts,
Bright with Thy praise,
Out of my strong griefs
Altars I'll raise;
So by my woes to be
Nearer, my God, to Thee!
Nearer to Thee!

And when on joyful wing
Cleaving the sky,
Sun, moon, and stars forgot,
Upward I fly;
Still all my song shall be
Nearer, my God, to Thee,
Nearer to Thee.

III.
L.M.

Jesus, and shall it ever be,
A mortal man ashamed of Thee:
Ashamed of Thee, whom angels praise,
Whose glories shine through endless days?

Ashamed of Jesus! Sooner far
Let night disown each radiant star;
'Tis midnight with my soul, till He,
Bright Morning Star, bid darkness flee.

Ashamed of Jesus! Oh, as soon
Let morning blush to own the sun;
He sheds the beams of light divine
O'er this benighted soul of mine.

Ashamed of Jesus! that dear Friend
On whom my hopes of heaven depend:
No; when I blush be this my shame,
That I no more revere his name.

Ashamed of Jesus! empty pride;
I'll boast a Saviour crucified;
And, oh, may this my portion be,
My Saviour not ashamed of me.

IV.

Almighty Father, unto Thee I call!
Make me submissive to Thy holy will:
Make me, though I should lose my earthly all
Obedient still.

Take me, unclean and sinful though I am,
And wash me in the blood of Christ, Thy Son:
O make my soul's unquiet surface calm;
Make me Thine own.

O make my heart Thy Spirit's resting place;
On me Thy blessing gently pour;
Make me at last to see thy glorious face,
And Thee adore.

Make me to fight the goodly fight of faith,
That when my earthly labors all shall cease,
May my eyelids gently close in death,
And rest in peace.

V.

Guide me, O Thou great Jehovah,
Pilgrim through this barren land;
I am weak, but Thou art mighty:
Hold me with Thy powerful hand.

Open now the crystal fountains
Whence the living waters flow;
Let the fiery, cloudy pillar
Lead me all my journey through.

Feed me with the heavenly manna
In this barren wilderness;
Be my sword, and shield, and banner;
Be the Lord my righteousness.

When I tread the verge of Jordan,
Bid my anxious fears subside;
Death of death, and hell's destruction
Land me safe on Canaan's side.

VI.

While Thee I seek, protecting Power,
Be my vain wishes stilled:
And may this consecrated hour
With better hopes be filled.

Thy love the power of thought bestowed,
To Thee my thoughts would soar;
Thy mercy o'er my life has flowed,
That mercy I adore.

In each event of life how clear
Thy ruling hand I see;
Each blessing to my soul more dear,
Because conferred by Thee.

In every joy that crowns my days,
In every pain I bear,
My heart shall find delight in praise,
Or seek relief in prayer.

When gladness wings my favored hour,
Thy love my thoughts shall fill;
Resigned when storms of sorrow lower,
My soul shall meet Thy will.

My lifted eye, without a tear,
The gathering storm shall see;
My steadfast heart shall know no fear.
That heart will rest on Thee.

VII.

Something, my God, for Thee—
Something for Thee!
That each day's setting sun may bring
Some penitential offering,

In thy dear name some kindness done—
To thy dear love some wanderer won—
Some trial meekly borne for Thee—
Dear Lord, for Thee.

Something, my God, for Thee—
Something for Thee!
That to thy gracious throne may rise
Sweet incense from some sacrifice;
Uplifted eyes undimmed by tears—
Uplifted faith unstained by fears,
Hailing each joy as light from Thee,
Dear Lord, from Thee.

Something, my God, for Thee—
Something for Thee!
For the great love that Thou hast given,
For the dear hope of Thee and heaven:
My soul her first allegiance brings,
And upward plumes her heavenward wings
Nearer, most gracious God, to Thee,
Nearer to Thee.

VIII.
C.M.

Oh! for a closer walk with God,
A calm and heavenly frame;
And light to shine upon the road
That leads me to the Lamb!

Where is the blessedness I knew
When first I saw the Lord?
Where is the soul-refreshing view
Of Jesus and his word?

What peaceful hours I once enjoyed!
How sweet their mem'ry still!
But they have left an aching void
The world can never fill.

Return, O holy Dove, return,
Sweet messenger of rest;
I hate the sins that made thee mourn.
And drove thee from my breast.

The dearest idol I have known,
Whate'er that idol be—
Help me to tear it from thy throne,
And worship only thee.

So shall my walk be close with God,
Calm and serene my frame;
And purer light shall mark the road
That leads me to the Lamb.

IX.
iii, 2.
Faith.

Rock of Ages, cleft for me,
Let me hide myself in Thee;
Let the water and the blood,
From thy side a healing flood,
Be of sin the double cure,
Save from wrath, and make me pure.

Should my tears for ever flow,
Should my zeal no languor know,
This for sin could not atone,
Thou must save, and Thou alone;
In my hand no price I bring,
Simply to Thy cross I cling.

While I draw this fleeting breath,
When my eyelids close in death,
When I rise to worlds unknown,

And behold Thee on Thy throne,
Rock of Ages, cleft for me,
Let me hide myself in Thee.

X.
4, 4.

How firm a foundation, ye saints of the Lord!
Is laid for your faith in his excellent word!
What more can he say, than to you he hath said—
You, who unto Jesus for refuge have fled?

Fear not, I am with thee, oh! be not dismayed,
I—I am thy God, and will still give thee aid;
I'll strengthen thee, help thee, and cause thee to stand,
Upheld by my righteous, omnipotent hand.

When through the deep waters I cause thee to go,
The rivers of sorrow shall not thee o'erflow;
For I will be with thee, thy troubles to bless,
And sanctify to thee thy deepest distress.

When through fiery trials thy pathway shall lie,
My grace all-sufficient shall be thy supply;
The flame shall not hurt thee—I only design
Thy dross to consume and thy gold to refine.

E'en down to old age, all my people shall prove
My sovereign, eternal, unchangeable love;
And when hoary hairs shall their temples adorn,
Like lambs they shall still in my bosom be borne.

The soul that on Jesus hath leaned for repose,
I will not, I **will** not, desert to his foes;
That soul, though all hell should endeavor to shake,
I'll never—no, never—no never forsake.

XI.
C. M.

Am I a soldier of the cross,
A follower of the Lamb,
And shall I fear to own his cause,
Or blush to speak his name?

Must I be carried to the skies,
On flowery beds of ease,
While others fought to win the prize,
And sailed through bloody seas?

Are there no foes for me to face?
Must I not stem the flood?
Is this dark world a friend to grace,
To help me on to God?

Sure I must fight, if I would reign;
Increase my courage, Lord;
I'll bear the toil, endure the pain,
Supported by thy word.

Thy saints in all this glorious war
Shall conquer, though they die;
They see the triumph from afar
With faith's discerning eye.

When that illustrious day shall rise,
And all thine armies shine
In robes of victory through the skies,
The glory shall be thine.

XII.

P. M.

I need thee, precious Jesus, for I am full of sin;
My soul is dark and guilty, my heart is dead within;
I need the cleansing fountain, where I can always flee—
The blood of Christ most precious, the sinner's perfect
plea.

I need thee, precious Jesus, I need a friend like thee—
A friend to soothe and sympathize, a friend to care for
me.
I need the heart of Jesus, to feel each anxious care,
To tell my every want, and all my sorrows share.

I need thee, precious Jesus, I need thee day by day,
To fill me with thy fulness, to lead me on my way;
I need thy holy spirit to teach me what I am,
To show me more of Jesus, to point me to the Lamb.

XIII.
L. M.

When I survey the wondrous cross
On which the Prince of Glory died,
My richest gain I count but loss,
And pour contempt on all my pride.

Forbid it, Lord, that I should boast,
Save in the cross of Christ my God:
All the vain things that charm me most,
I sacrifice them to thy blood.

See! from his head, his hands, his feet
Sorrow and love flow mingled down:
Did e'er such love and sorrow meet?
Or thorns compose a Saviour's crown?

Were the whole realm of nature mine,
That were a tribute far too small;
Love so amazing, so divine,
Demands my life, my soul, my all.

XIV.
C. M.

How sweet the name of Jesus sounds
In a believer's ear!
It soothes his sorrows, heals his wounds,
And drives away his fear.

It makes the wounded spirit whole,
And calms the troubled breast;
'T is manna to the hungry soul,
And to the weary, rest.

By Him my prayers acceptance gain,
Although with sin defiled;
Satan accuses me in vain,
And I am owned a child.

Weak is the effort of my heart,
And cold my warmest thought;
But when I see Thee as Thou art,
I'll praise Thee as I ought.

Till then I would Thy love proclaim
With every fleeting breath:
And may the music of thy name
Refresh my soul in death.

XV.
L. M.

"Him that cometh unto me I will in nowise cast him out." [John 6:37]

Just as I am—without one plea,
But that Thy blood was shed for me,
And that Thou bid'st me come to Thee,
O Lamb of God, I come.

Just as I am—and waiting not
To rid my soul of one dark blot—
To Thee, whose blood can cleanse each spot.
O Lamb of God, I come.

Just as I am—though tossed about
With many a conflict, many a doubt,
With fears within, and foes without—
O Lamb of God, I come.

Just as I am—poor, wretched, blind—
Sight, riches, healing of the mind,
Yea, all I need, in Thee to find,
O Lamb of God, I come.

Just as I am—Thou wilt receive,
Wilt welcome, pardon, cleanse, relieve,
Because Thy promise I believe—
O Lamb of God, I come.

Just as I am—Thy love unknown
Has broken every barrier down:
Now to be Thine, yea, Thine alone,
O Lamb of God, I come.

XVI.
Love.

My God, I love Thee! not because
I hope for heaven thereby;
Nor yet because if I love not
I must for ever die.

But, O my Jesus, Thou didst me
Upon Thy cross embrace;
For me didst bear the nails and spear,
And manifold disgrace;

And griefs and torments numberless;
And sweat of agony;
E'en death itself; and all for one
Who was Thine enemy.

Then why, O blessed Jesus Christ!
Should I not love Thee well;
Not for the sake of winning heaven,
Or of escaping hell;

Not for the hope of gaining aught;
Not seeking a reward;
But as Thyself hast loved me,
O ever-loving Lord?

E'en so I love Thee, and will love,
And in Thy praise will sing;
Solely because Thou art my God,
And my eternal King.

XVII.

Lord, with glowing heart I'd praise Thee
For the bliss Thy love bestows;
For the pardoning grace that saves me,
And the peace that from it flows:
Help, O God, my weak endeavor;
This dull soul to rapture raise:
Thou must light the flame, or never
Can my love be warmed to praise.

Praise, my soul, the God that sought thee,
Wretched wanderer, far astray;
Found thee lost, and kindly brought thee
From the paths of death away;
Praise, with love's devoutest feeling,
Him who saw thy guilt-born fear,
And, the light of hope revealing,
Bade the blood-stained cross appear.

Lord, this bosom's ardent feeling
Vainly would my lips express;
Low before Thy footstool kneeling,
Deign Thy suppliant's prayer to bless:
Let Thy grace, my soul's chief treasure,
Love's pure flame within me raise;
And, since words can never measure,
Let my life show forth Thy praise.

XVIII.
C. M.

Jesus, I love Thy charming name;
'T is music to mine ear;
Fain would I sound it out so loud
That earth and heaven should hear.

Yes, Thou art precious to my soul,
My joy, my hope, my trust;
Jewels to Thee are gaudy toys,
And gold is sordid dust.

Thy grace still dwells upon my heart,
And sheds its fragrance there;
The noblest balm of all its wounds,
The cordial of its care.

I'll speak the honors of Thy name
With my last laboring breath;
Then speechless clasp Thee in mine arms,
The antidote of death.

XIX.
S. M.
Worship.

Welcome sweet day of rest
That saw the Lord arise;
Welcome to this reviving breast,
And these rejoicing eyes.

The King himself comes near,
To feast his saints to-day;
Here may we sit and see Him here,
And love, and praise, and pray.

One day amidst the place
Where Jesus is within,
Is better than ten thousand days
Of pleasure and of sin.

My willing soul would stay
In such a frame as this,
Till it is called to soar away
To everlasting bliss.

XX.
C. M.

Come, Holy Spirit, heavenly Dove,
With all thy quickening powers,
Kindle a frame of sacred love
In these cold hearts of ours.

Look, how we grovel here below,
Fond of these trifling toys!
Our souls can neither fly nor go
To reach eternal joys.

In vain we tune our formal songs;
In vain we strive to rise;
Hosannas languish on our tongues,
And our devotion dies.

Dear Lord! and shall we ever live
At this poor, dying rate?
Our love so faint, so cold to thee,
And thine to us so great.

Come, Holy Spirit, heavenly Dove,
With all thy quickening powers!
Come, shed abroad a Saviour's love,
And that shall kindle ours.

XXI.
L. M.

My God, permit me not to be
A stranger to myself and Thee;
Amidst a thousand thoughts I rove,
Forgetful of my highest love.

Why should my passions mix with earth,
And thus debase my heavenly birth;
Why should I cleave to things below,
And let my God, my Saviour go?

Call me away from flesh and sense,
One sovereign word can draw me thence;
I would obey the voice divine,
And all inferior joys resign.

Be earth with all her scenes withdrawn;
Let noise and vanity be gone:
In secret silence of the mind,
My heaven, and there my God, I find.

XXII.
L. M.

Where high the heavenly temple stands,
The house of God not made with hands,
A great High Priest our nature wears—
The Guardian of mankind appears.

Though now ascended up on high,
He bends on earth a brother's eye;
Partaker of the human name,
He knows the frailty of our frame.

Our Fellow-sufferer yet retains
A fellow-feeling of our pains;
And still remembers, in the skies,
His tears, his agonies, and cries.

In every pang that rends the heart
The Man of sorrow had a part;
He sympathizes in our grief,
And to the sufferer sends relief.

With boldness, therefore, at the throne,
Let us make all our sorrows known;
And ask the aid of heavenly power
To help us in the evil hour.

XXIII.
S. M.

Come ye that love the Lord,
And let your joys be known;
Join in a song with sweet accord,
And thus surround the throne.

Children of grace have found
Glory began below:
Celestial fruits on earthly ground
From faith and hope may grow.

The hill of Sion yields
A thousand sacred sweets,
Before we reach the heavenly fields,
Or walk the golden streets.

Then let our songs abound,
And every tear be dry;
We're travelling through Immanuel's ground,
To fairer worlds on high.

XXIV.
C. M.
Prayer.

Approach, my soul, the mercy seat,
Where Jesus answers prayer;
There humbly fall before his feet,
For none can perish there.

Thy promise is my only plea,
With this I venture nigh;
Thou callest burdened souls to Thee,
And such, O Lord, am I.

Bowed down beneath a load of sin,
By Satan sorely pressed,
By war without, and fear within,
I come to Thee for rest.

Be Thou my shield and hiding place;
That, sheltered near Thy side,
I may my fierce accuser face,
And tell him "Thou hast died!"

Oh, wondrous love to bleed and die,
To bear the cross and shame,
That guilty sinners, such as I,
Might plead Thy gracious name.

XXV.
C. M.

Prayer is the soul's sincere desire,
Uttered or unexpressed;
The motion of a hidden fire
That trembles in the breast.

Prayer is the burden of a sigh,
The falling of a tear;
The upward glancing of an eye,
When none but God is near.

Prayer is the simplest form of speech
That infant lips can try;
Prayer the sublimest strains that reach
The Majesty on high.

Prayer is the Christian's vital breath,
The Christian's native air,
The watchword at the gates of death;
He enters heaven with prayer.

Prayer is the contrite sinner's voice,
Returning from his ways;
While angels in their songs rejoice,
And cry, "Behold, he prays!"

In prayer, on earth, the saints are one;
They're one in word and mind,
When with the Father and the Son
Sweet fellowship they find.

O Thou, by whom we come to God,
The life, the truth, the way,
The path of prayer thyself hast trod,
Lord, teach us how to pray.

XXVI.
C. M.
Providence.

Angels, where'er we go, attend
Our steps, whate'er betide;
With watchful care their charge defend,
And evil turn aside.

Myriads of bright cherubic bands,
Sent by the King of kings,
Rejoice to bear us in their hands,
And shade us with their wings.

Jehovah's charioteers surround;
The ministerial choir
Encamp where'er His heirs are found,
And form our wall of fire.

Ten thousand offices unseen
For us they gladly do,
Deliver in the furnace keen,
And safe escort us through.

And thronging round, with steadfast love,
They guard the dying breast,
The lurking fiend far off remove,
And soothe our souls to rest;

And when our spirits we resign,
On outstretched wings they bear,
And lodge us in the arms divine,
And leave us ever there.

XXVII.
3, 1.

"My times are in Thy hand." [Psalm 31:15]

Sovereign Ruler of the skies,
Ever gracious, ever wise,
All our times are in thy hand,
All events at thy command.

He that formed us in the womb,
He shall guide us to the tomb;
All our ways shall ever be
Ordered by His wise decree.

Times of sickness, times of health,
Blighting want, and cheerful wealth,
All our pleasures, all our pains,
Come and end as God ordains.

May we always own Thy hand,
Still to Thee surrendered stand,
Know that Thou art God alone,
We and ours are all Thy own!

XXVIII.
C. M.

God moves in a mysterious way
His wonders to perform;
He plants his footsteps in the sea,
And rides upon the storm.

Judge not the Lord by feeble sense,
But trust him for his grace:
Behind a frowning providence
He hides a smiling face.

His purposes will ripen fast,
Unfolding every hour:
The bud may have a bitter taste,
But sweet will be the flower.

Blind unbelief is sure to err,
And scan his work in vain;
God is his own interpreter,
And He will make it plain.

XXIX.
C. M.
Redemption.

There is a fountain filled with blood,
Drawn from Immanuel's veins;
And sinners plunged beneath that flood
Leave all their guilty stains.

The dying thief rejoiced to see
That fountain in his day;
And there may I, though vile as he,
Wash all my sins away.

Dear, dying Lamb, Thy precious blood
Shall never lose its power,
Till all the ransom'd Church of God
Be saved, to sin no more.

E'er since, by faith, I saw the stream
Thy flowing wounds supply,
Redeeming love has been my theme,
And shall be till I die.

Then in a nobler, sweeter song,
I'll sing Thy power to save;
When this poor, lisping, stamm'ring tongue
Lies silent in the grave.

XXX.
C. M.

To our Redeemer's glorious name
Awake the sacred song!
O may his love, immortal flame,
Tune every heart and tongue.

His love what mortal thought can reach,
What mortal tongue display;
Imagination's utmost stretch
In wonder dies away.

He left his radiant throne on high;
Left the bright realms of bliss;
And came to earth to bleed and die:
Was ever love like this?

Dear Lord, while we adoring pay
Our humble thanks to Thee,
May every heart with rapture say:
The Saviour died for me.

O may the sweet, the blissful theme,
Fill every heart and tongue,
Till strangers love Thy charming name,
And join the sacred song.

XXXI.
C. M.

Salvation! O the joyful sound!
Glad tidings to our ears;
A sovereign balm for every wound,
A cordial for our fears.

Salvation! buried once by sin,
At hell's dark door we lay,
But now we rise by grace divine,
And see a heavenly day.

Salvation! let the echo fly
The spacious earth around,
While all the armies of the sky
Conspire to raise the sound.

Salvation! O thou bleeding Lamb,
To Thee the praise belongs;
Our hearts shall kindle at Thy name,
Thy name inspire our songs.

CHORUS.

Glory, honor, praise, and power
Be unto the Lamb for ever;
Jesus Christ is our Redeemer;
Hallelujah, praise the Lord.

XXXII.
P. M.
Judgment.

DIES IRAE.

Day of wrath! that day of mourning,
See once more the cross returning,
Heaven and earth in ashes burning.

O what fear man's bosom rendeth,
When from heaven the Judge descendeth,
On whose sentence all dependeth!

Lo! the trumpet's wondrous swelling,
Peals through each sepulchral dwelling,
All before the throne compelling.

Death is struck, and nature quaking,
All creation is awaking,
To its Judge an answer making.

Lo! the book exactly worded!
Wherein all hath been recorded;
Thence shall judgment be awarded.

When the Judge his seat attaineth,
And each hidden deed arraigneth,
Nothing unavenged remaineth.

What shall I, frail man, be pleading?
Who for me be interceding
When the just are mercy needing.

King of majesty tremendous,
Who dost free salvation send us,
Fount of pity! then befriend us.

Think, kind Jesus, my salvation
Cost Thy wondrous incarnation;
Leave me not to reprobation!

Faint and weary Thou hast sought me,
On the cross of suff'ring bought me;
Shall such grace in vain be brought me?

Righteous Judge of retribution,
Grant thy gift of absolution,
Ere that day's dread execution.

Guilty, now I pour my moaning,
All my shame with anguish owing;
Spare, O God, thy suppliant groaning!

Thou the harlot gav'st remission,
Heard'st the dying thief's petition;
Hopeless else were my condition.

Worthless are my prayers and sighing,
Yet, good Lord, in grace complying,
Rescue me from fires undying!

With Thy favored sheep, O place me!
Nor among the goats abase me;
But to Thy right hand upraise me.

While the wicked are confounded,
Doomed to flames of woe unbounded,
Call me with Thy saints surrounded.

Bow my heart in meek submission
Strewn with ashes of contrition—
Succor Thou my lost condition.

Day of sorrows, day of weeping,
When in dust no longer sleeping,
Man awakes in Thy dread keeping.

To the rest Thou didst prepare him
On Thy cross, O Christ, upbear him:
Spare, O God, in mercy spare him.

XXXIII.
P. M.
Our Rest.

"The sufferings of this present time are not worthy to be compared to the glory that shall be revealed in us." [Romans 8:18]

My feet are worn and weary with the march
Over rough roads and up the steep hill-side;
O! city of our God, I fain would see
Thy pastures green where peaceful waters glide.

My hands are weary, laboring, toiling on,
Day after day, for perishable meat;
Oh! city of our God, I fain would rest;
I sigh to gain thy glorious mercy seat.

My garments, travel-worn, and stained with dust,
Oft rent by briars and thorns that crowd my way,
Would fain be made, O Lord, my righteousness,
Spotless and white in heaven's unclouded ray.

My eyes are weary looking at the sin,
Impiety, and scorn upon the earth;
Oh! city of our God, within Thy walls.
All, all are clothed upon with the new birth.

My heart is weary of its own deep sin—
Sinning, repenting, sinning still alway;
When shall my soul thy glorious presence feel,
And find its guilt, dear Saviour, washed away.

Patience, poor soul; thy Saviour's feet were worn;
The Saviour's heart and hands were weary too;
His garments stained, and travel-worn, and old;
His sacred eyes blinded with tears for you.

Love thou the path of sorrow that He trod,
Toil on, and wait in patience for thy rest;
Oh! city of our God, we soon shall see
Thy glorious halls, home of the loved and blest.

XXXIV.
P. M.
God's Support and Guidance.

Forsake me not, my God,
Thou God of my salvation!
Give me Thy light, to be
My sure illumination.
My soul to folly turns,
Seeking she knows not what;
Oh! lead her to Thyself—
My God, forsake me not!

Forsake me not, my God!
Take not Thy spirit from me;
And suffer not the might
Of sin to overcome me.
A father pitieth
The children he begot;
My Father, pity me;
My God, forsake me not!

Forsake me not, my God!
Thou God of life and power,
Enliven, strengthen me,
In every evil hour;
And when the sinful fire
Within my heart is hot,
Be not Thou far from me;
My God, forsake me not!

Forsake me not, my God!
Uphold me in my going,
That evermore I may
Please Thee in all well doing;
And that Thy will, O Lord,
May never be forgot
In all my works and ways—
My God, forsake me not!

Forsake me not, my God!
I would be Thine for ever;
Confirm me mightily
In every right endeavor.
And when my hour is come,
Cleansed from all stain and spot
Of sin, receive my soul;
My God, forsake me not!

XXXV.
P. M.
Jesus our Hope and Trust.

Jesus lives, and so shall I:
Death! thy sting is gone for ever!
He who deigned for me to die,
Lives the bands of death to sever.
He shall raise me with the just:
Jesus is my Hope and Trust.

Jesus lives and reigns supreme;
And, His kingdom still remaining,
I shall also be with Him,
Ever living, ever reigning,
God has promised; be it must:
Jesus is my Hope and Trust.

Jesus lives, and God extends
Grace to each returning sinner;
Rebels he receives as friends,
And exalts to highest honor.
God is true, as he is just:
Jesus is my Hope and Trust.

Jesus lives, and by His grace
Victory o'er my passions giving,
I will cleanse my heart and ways,

Ever to His glory living.
The weak He raises from the dust;
Jesus is my Hope and Trust.

Jesus lives, and I am sure
Naught shall me from Jesus sever.
Satan's wiles and Satan's power,
Pain or pleasure—ye shall never!
Christian armor can not rust:
Jesus is my Hope and Trust.

Jesus lives, and death is now
But my entrance into glory.
Courage! then, my soul, for thou
Hast a crown of life before thee:
Thou shalt find thy hopes were just,
Jesus is the Christian's Trust.

XXXVI.
4, 4.
I would not live alway.

I would not live alway—live alway below!
O, no! I'll not linger when bidden to go.
The days of our pilgrimage granted us here
Are enough for life's woes, full enough for its cheer.

Would I shrink from the path which the prophets of
God,
Apostles and martyrs, so joyfully trod?
While brethren and friends are all hastening home,
Like a spirit unblest o'er the earth would I roam?

I would not live alway—I ask not to stay,
Where storm after storm rises dark o'er the way;
Where, seeking for peace, we but hover around
Like the patriarch's bird, and no resting is found;
Where hope, when she paints her gay bow on the air,
Leaves its brilliance to fade in the night of despair,
And joy's fleeting angel ne'er sheds a glad ray,
Save the gleam of the plumage that bears him away.

I would not live alway—thus fettered by sin,
Temptation without, and corruption within;
In a moment of strength, if I sever the chain,
Scarce the victory is mine, ere I'm captive again.
E'en the rapture of pardon is mingled with fears,
And my cup of thanksgiving with penitent tears:

The festival trump calls for jubilant songs,
But my spirit her own miserere prolongs.

I would not live alway—no, welcome the tomb;
Immortality's lamp burns there bright 'mid the gloom;
There, too, is the pillow, where Christ bowed his head;
O soft are the slumbers on that holy bed!
And then the glad dawn soon to follow that night,
When the sunrise of glory shall beam on my sight,
When the full matin song, as the sleepers arise
To shout in the morning, shall peal through the skies.

Who, who would live alway? away from his God,
Away from yon heaven, that blissful abode,
Where the rivers of pleasure flow o'er the bright plains,
And the noontide of glory eternally reigns;
Where the saints of all ages in harmony meet,
Their Saviour and brethren transported to greet,
While the songs of salvation unceasingly roll,
And the smile of the Lord is the feast of the soul.

That heavenly music! what is it I hear?
The notes of the harpers ring sweet in the air:
And see, soft unfolding those portals of gold;
The King all arrayed in his beauty behold!
O give me, O give me the wings of a dove!
Let me hasten my flight to those mansions above;
Ay, 't is now that my soul on swift pinions would soar,
And in ecstacy bid earth adieu evermore.

XXXVII.
7s.
Invitation and Warning.

Sinners, turn, why will ye die?
God, your Maker, asks you why:
God, who did your being give,
Made you with Himself to live:
He the fatal cause demands,
Asks the works of His own hands:
Why, ye thankless creatures, why
Will ye cross His love and die?

Sinners, turn, why will ye die?
God, your Saviour, asks you why:
He, who did your souls retrieve,
Died himself that ye might live.
Will you let him die in vain?
Crucify your Lord again?
Why, ye ransomed sinners, why
Will ye slight his grace, and die?

Sinners, turn, why will ye die?
God, the Spirit, asks you why:
He who all your lives hath strove,
Wooed you to embrace his love.

Will ye not His grace receive?
Will ye still refuse to live?
O, ye dying sinners, why,
Why will ye for ever die?

XXXVIII.
S. M.
Rev. xxii, 17-20.

The Spirit, in our hearts,
Is whispering, sinner, come:
The Bride, the Church of Christ, proclaims
To all his children, come.

Let him that heareth say
To all about him, come:
Let him that thirsts for righteousness,
To Christ, the fountain, come.

Yes, whosoever will,
O let him freely come
And freely drink the stream of life:
'T is Jesus bids him come.

Lo, Jesus, who invites,
Declares, I quickly come.
Lord! even so; I wait thy hour:
Jesus, my Saviour come.

XXXIX.

There is a land of pure delight,
Where saints immortal reign;
Eternal day excludes the night,
And pleasures banish pain.

There everlasting spring abides,
And never-fading flowers;
Death, like a narrow sea, divides
This heavenly land from ours.

Bright fields, beyond the swelling flood
Stand dressed in living green;
So to the Jews fair Canaan stood,
While Jordan rolled between.

Could we but climb where Moses stood,
And view the landscape o'er,
Not Jordan's stream, nor death's cold flood,
Should fright us from the shore.

XL.
For the Hospital.

When languor and disease invade
This trembling house of clay,
'T is sweet to look by faith abroad,
And long to flee away.

Sweet to look inward, and attend
The whispers of his love;
Sweet to look upward to the throne
When Jesus pleads above.

Sweet on his faithfulness to rest,
Whose love can never end;
Sweet on the promise of his grace,
For all things to depend.

XLI.
For a Funeral.

Hear what the voice from heaven declares
To those in Christ who die!
"Released from all their earthly cares,
They'll reign with him on high."

Then why lament departed friends,
Or shake at death's alarms?
Death's but the servant Jesus sends
To call us to His arms.

If sin be pardoned, we're secure,
Death hath no sting beside;
The law gave sin its strength and power;
But Christ, our ransom, died!

Then joyfully, while life we have,
To Christ our life we'll sing,
"Where is thy victory, O grave?
And where, O death, thy sting?"

XLII.
S. M.

And will the Judge descend,
And must the dead arise,
And not a single soul escape
His all-discerning eyes;

And from His righteous lips
Shall the dread sentence sound,
And through the numerous guilty throng
Spread black despair around?

Depart from me, accursed,
To everlasting flame,
For rebel angels first prepared
Where mercy never came.

How will my heart endure
The terrors of that day,
When earth and heaven before His face
Astonished shrink away.

But, ere the trumpet shakes
The mansions of the dead,
Hark from the Gospel's cheering sound
What joyful tidings spread.

Ye sinners, seek His grace,
Whose wrath ye can not bear;
Fly to the shelter of the Cross,
And find salvation there.

So shall that curse remove,
By which the Saviour bled,
And the last awful day shall pour
His blessings on your head.

XLIII.
L. M.
The Christian's Death.

Asleep in Jesus! oh, how sweet,
To be for such a slumber meet;
With holy confidence to sing,
That death hath lost its painful sting.

Asleep in Jesus! peaceful rest!
Whose waking is supremely blest;
No fear, no woe, shall dim the hour
That manifests the Saviour's power.

Asleep in Jesus! far from thee
Thy kindred and their graves may be;
But thine is still a blessed sleep,
From which none ever wakes to weep.

XLIV.
Another.

Servant of God, well done!
Go forth from earth's employ,
The battle fought, the victory won,
Enter thy Master's joy.

At midnight came the cry,
"To meet thy God prepare!"
He woke—and caught his Captain's eye,
Still strong in faith and prayer.

Soldier of Christ, well done,
Praise be thy new employ;
And while eternal ages run,
Rest in thy Saviour's joy.

BALM FOR THE WEARY AND THE WOUNDED

BY
REV. C.T. QUINTARD,

Chaplain 1st Tenn. Reg't, C.S.A.

COLUMBIA

"O Father! not my will, but Thine be done,"
So spake the Son.
Be this our charm, mellowing earth's ruder noise
Of griefs and joys;
That we may cling for ever to Thy breast
In perfect rest!

PREFACE.

The following work has been arranged for such of our soldiers as have, by reason of wounds or disease, been compelled to exchange active service in the field for the harder and more wearying service in the hospital, or on the bed of sickness and pain.

If it be true that—"They also serve, who only stand and wait," surely they serve who suffer and endure. Sickness is as truly a "state of life into which it pleases God to call us" as is health, and it is to be used for the same end—His glory, and our own good. Suffering, endurance, whether of pain or trials, is as much a vocation as is the full exercise of the powers of mind and body in the active duties of life. It is what God calls us to—it is His work, and He will bless it. It may be the work of lying still, of not stirring hand or foot, of scarcely speaking, scarcely showing life. Still it is His work.

Some must suffer, and some must serve; but each one is necessary to the other; "the whole body is fitly framed together by that which every joint supplieth."

Some learn more quickly in the school of sickness and sorrow than others, because they take great pains to learn, and are never satisfied with present progress; they are ever seeking to know more, to practice more, to rise higher. Our soldiers know very well how to labor and do for their country, and they can certainly learn to wait and to endure. Let them resolve to bear their trials, of every sort, with manly fortitude, and employ their periods of retirement and suffering in laying, broad and deep, the foundations of a genuine Christian character, and they will never lack the most efficient means of promoting our national independence.

DEUS NOSTER REFUGIUM.

IN MEMORIAM

This little manual is inscribed to the memory of Captain THOMAS EDWARD KING, of Roswell, Georgia, who fell at the Battle of Chickamauga, on Saturday, the 19th day of September, A.D. 1863.

His life was rendered illustrious by an exhibition of all those virtues which adorn the patriot and the Christian.

He was brave without temerity, generous without prodigality, noble without pride, and virtuous without severity.

Wounded at the Battle of Manassas, on the 21st of July, 1861, he was unable to resume the command of his company; but when his native state was threatened he felt that he must "join the struggle to drive the invader from his altar and his home." He accepted a position on the staff of the gallant General Preston Smith, and fell with him, at the close of the day, cheerfully offering up his life for his country's cause. The sanctity of home-life may not be invaded, or we should find there such a display of love, generosity, and large-heartedness as would at once give charm, and dignity, and grace to all its relations. But, in every position in which he was placed or called upon to act, he exhibited, from the dawn of life to its close, the same high qualities—

"The childhood shows the man,
As morning shows the day."

He was a son who never drew a father's tear. He was a patriot who consecrated all the energies of soul and body to his country, and laid down life itself for its defense.

He was a Christian with a heart full of sympathy for every sorrow, and who recognized the connection of our highest hopes in heaven with our tenderest charities in earthly life. He had visions of God through purity of heart, and the life of God upon earth was the antechamber of that eternity of God upon which he has entered. My heart went with him to the battle-field, and, ever and anon, as the deathful volleys echoed on my ear, I prayed that he might be spared. It was not to be; and, when he fell, I had been more than man had I not felt my heartstrings tear.

The perishable heart, in its passionate yearning for the perishable, must bleed; and mine bled as I bore his body from the field of carnage and death. But the immortal, redeemed, regenerated, and renewed is healed and comforted in its love of the Immortal. The cross of Christ to which it clings lifts it above the world. It can say: "The Lord gave, and the Lord hath taken away." And it can say, also: "BLESSED BE THE NAME OF THE LORD."

"His bosom, with one death-shot riven,
The warrior lay low;
His face was turned unto the heaven,
His feet unto the foe.

"As he had fallen upon the plain,
Inviolate he lay;
No ruffian spoiler's hand profane,
Had touched that noble clay.

"And precious things he still retained,
Which, by one distant hearth,
Loved tokens of the loved, had gained
A worth beyond all worth.

"I treasured these for them who yet
Knew not their mighty woe;
I softly sealed his eyes, and set
One kiss upon his brow."
—Trench.

In Christ's eternal kingdom the distinction will be, who is the most like Him who has done his work most faithfully. ... It is a comfort to reflect that our Heavenly Father knows all the circumstances of our trial, and appreciates every effort and every desire for sanctification and improvement. ... We have nothing to do with His arrangements; He sets us our work; we have to do it; step by step, day by day, be it little or much, it matters not, so that we are but faithful; it will all fit, in some wonderful way, into His great plan.

—Brampton Rectory.

The skirmish may be sharp, but it can not last long. The cloud, while it drops, is passing over thy head; then comes fair weather, and an eternal sunshine of glory.

—Gurnall's Christian Armor.

...Casting all your care upon Him, for He careth for you... [1 Peter 5:7]

What a calm, what a peace in the midst of a storm, does this gracious habit of godly dependence give to a man! Suppose, tomorrow, that you were expecting something very important to take place, and a heavy burden of care is the natural consequence of so grave an expectation. You are calm and composed; your mind is at peace. You have done your best to meet the emergency, and, as a Christian, as a man of God, you cast all your care upon Him, knowing assuredly that He careth for you. And there is really a to-morrow of importance to every one of us. We shall have to unloose the bands of mortality. We shall have to take off our outer garments, and, bidding good-night to all about our strange and narrow bed, we shall have to lie down for the last time on earth, and let death put out our light. Oh! what a happy thing it will be for Faith, the handmaid of the Lord, to sound in our ear for the last time: "Casting all your care upon Him," and for us to reply: "Yes! yes! He careth for us!" and then to fall asleep.

—Sermon by Rev. J. Hullett.

My lifted eye, without a tear,
The gathering storm shall see;
My trembling heart shall own no fear
While it can trust in Thee.
—Anon.

There is an unseen battle-field
In every human breast,
Where two opposing forces meet,
And where they seldom rest.

That field is veiled from mortal sight;
'T is only seen by One
Who knows alone where victory lies,
When each day's fight is done.

One army clusters strong and fierce,
Their chief of demon form:
His brow is like the thunder-cloud,
His voice, the bursting storm.

His Captains —Pride, and Lust, and Hate—
Whose troops watch night and day,
Swift to detect the weakest point,
And thirsting for the prey.

Contending with this mighty force,
Is but a little band;
Yet there, with an unquailing front,
Those warriors firmly stand!

Their leader is God-like form,
Of countenance serene;
And glowing on His loving breast,
A naked cross is seen.

His Captains —Faith, and Hope, and Love—
Point to that wondrous sign;
And gazing on it, all receive
Strength from a source Divine.

They feel it speaks a glorious truth,
A truth as great as sure—
That to be victors they must learn
To love, confide, endure.

That faith sublime, in wildest strife,
Imparts a holy calm;
For every deadly blow a shield,
For every wound a balm.

And when they win the battlefield,
Past toil is quite forgot;
That plain were carnage once had reigned,
Becomes a hallowed spot:

A spot where flowers of joy and peace
Spring from the fertile sod,
And breathe the perfume of their praise
On every breeze—to God.
—Anon.

Whatever be the intensity of sorrow that bows and presses the heart of man, remember that, for every grief you suffer, the meek and Holy One suffered a thousand—that there is not in the spirit a dungeon or recess of anguish, however untrodden or lonely, in which the Lord of glory was not a mourning inhabitant before you. Does the victim know the loss of earthly comforts? Christ knew not where to lay his head. Does he regret the fall from wealth or power? Let him remember who it was that emptied himself of glory which he had before the world was, and left the throne of the universe for the agonies of Calvary. Does he deplore the loss of friends? Christ was friendless in his most trying hour. Does he bewail the ingratitude of friends? Christ was betrayed by his own familiar one. Finally, does he fear the coming of death—the torture of the separation? What death can we anticipate which shall approach the horror of the last days of his Redeemer? Thus, wherever we turn, whatever be our shade of grief, we are but feeble copyists of the great sufferer, who, in His own person, exhausted every variety of human sorrow.

—Archer Butler.

Christ leads me through no darker rooms
Than He went through before;
He that unto Christ's kingdom comes,
Must enter by His door.

Come, Lord, when grace has made me meet
Thy blessed face to see;

For if Thy work on earth be sweet,
What will Thy glory be?
—Baxter.

My daughter, do not imagine that the work of your
sanctification will be an easy one. Cherry-trees bear fruit
soon after they are planted, but that fruit is small and
perishable: while the palm, the prince of trees, requires a
hundred years before it is mature enough to bring forth
dates. A lukewarm degree of piety may be acquired in a
year; but the perfection to which we aspire, oh, my dear
daughter, must be the growth of long and weary years.
—Jacqueline Pascal.

From strength to strength go on,
Wrestle, and fight, and pray;
Tread all the powers of darkness down,
And win the well-fought day.
—Hymn.

Strive to realize the abiding presence of Christ with all his
children, and personally with yourselves. When you rise in
the morning, rise to His companionship. In the little
duties of the day imagine Him by your side, and act as
with His eye upon you. See in your daily mercies an
evidence of His love, and for those mercies thank and
praise Him with your lips and your lives. As He loves you,
so, from his example, learn to love and labor for those
around you. You, as Christians, are to do Christ's work in
the sphere in which He as placed you. You are to show, in

your character and conduct, the fruits of His religion—gentleness, goodness, meekness, temperance, faith. These are the virtues which, exemplified in you, will draw others to walk in the path that you are treading; and with the desire to please Him, you will find sufficient opportunities. To the poor, you may be as ministers of mercy; to your younger sisters, as winning guides; to your companions and friends, as persuasive illustrations of the beauty of holiness. Not that you will attain to this at once. Temptations and discouragements will come to you as to every one, but prayer and perseverance are remedies for all. The straight and narrow way is no flowery path. Flowers do not blossom there more beautiful and fragrant than any which the world can offer. But they grow in the clefts of the rocks which we climb, and in the depths of the valleys where we must descend. Yet, as we travel on that road, it becomes more easy and more peaceful. Heaven's sunshine streams over it, and heaven's glory is beyond. And, when the goal at last is reached, we shall regret no labor, shall grieve over no sacrifice that has been made for the sake of Christ, and that has gained for us His welcome: "Well done, good and faithful servant."

—The Sisters Clare preparing for Confirmation.

I suppose the great temptation to which we are, more or less, exposed, is that of losing sight of God in the ordinary actions of the day. It is hard to feel that every action of every day is capable of being so done as to advance or hinder our salvation, and yet nothing surely can be more

evident. St. Paul says that, whether we eat or drink, or whatever we do, we are to do all to the glory of God, and in His name. This, no doubt, is a strict rule, and yet it is also one full of consolation—for it shows us how entirely the life of true religion is within the reach and power of every one of us. If we really traced every blessing we received to God, and at the same time referred all our trials and sorrows to Him also, ever looking upon him as the one great Cause of all that befalls us, and regarding man as his instrument only, how much of sin, ingratitude, and folly should we escape.
—The Life of Faith.

When I can trust my all with God,
In trial's fearful hour,
Bow, all resign'd, beneath his rod,
And bless his sparing power;
A joy springs up amid distress,
A fountain in the wilderness.

O, to be brought to Jesus' feet,
Through sorrows fix me there,
Is still a privilege; and sweet
The energies of prayer,
Though sighs and tears its language be,
If Christ be nigh and smile on me.

O, blessed be the hand that gave,
Still blessed when it takes;
Blessed be He who smites to save,

Who heals the heart He breaks;
Perfect and true are all His ways,
Whom heaven adores and earth obeys.

The work of our sanctification consists simply in receiving, from one moment to another, all the troubles and duties of our state in life as veils under which God hides himself, and gives himself to us. Every moment brings some duty to be faithfully performed, and this is enough for our perfection. The moment which brings a duty to be performed, or a trouble to be borne, brings also a message declaring to us the will of God.
—The Life of Faith.

The good Christian is not one who has no inclination to sin (for we have all the seed of sin in us); but who, being sensible of such inclinations, denieth them continually, and suffers them not to grow into evil actions.

Every day deny yourself some satisfaction; your eyes, objects of mere curiosity; your tongue, every thing that may feed vanity or vent enmity; the palate, dainties; the ears, flattery, and whatever corrupts the heart; the body, ease and luxury; bearing all the inconveniences of life for the love of God—cold, hunger, restless nights, ill health, unwelcome news, the faults of servants, contempt, ingratitude of friends, malice of enemies, calumnies, our own failings, lowness of spirits, the struggle in overcoming our corruptions—bearing all these with patience and resignation **to** the will of God. Do all this as unto God, with the greatest privacy.

All ways are indifferent to one who has heaven in his eye, as a traveller does not choose the pleasantest but the shortest and safest way to his journey's end; and that is the way of the Cross which Jesus Christ made choice of, and sanctified it to His followers.

God does not require it of us that we should not feel any uneasiness under the Cross, but that we should strive to overcome it by His grace.
—Bishop Wilson.

Each cross hath its inscription.
—Proverb.

Who loves the cross, and Him who on it died,
In every cloud sees Jesus by his side. The Divine Master.

Take thou thy cross, my son; nor mayest thou choose;
The cross When I can trust my all with God I give is best—do not refuse. The Divine Master.

I weep, but do not yield; I mourn, yet still rebel;
My inmost soul seems steel'd, cold, and immovable.
The wound is sharp and deep; my spirit bleeds within;
And yet I lie asleep, and still I sin, I sin.

My bruised soul complains of stripes without, within;
I feel those piercing pains—yet still I sin, I sin.
O'er me the low cloud hangs its weight of shade and fear;
Unmoved I pass along, and still my sin is here.

Yon massive mountain peak the lightening [sic] rends at
    will;
The rock can melt or break—I am unbroken still.
My sky was once noon-bright, my day was calm the
    while;
I loved the pleasant light, the sunshine's happy smile.

I said, my God, O, sure this love will kindle mine;
Let but this calm endure, then all my heart is thine.
Alas! I knew it not! the summer flung its gold
Of sunshine o'er my lot, and yet my heart was cold.

Trust me with prosperous days, I said, O spare the rod;
Thee and Thy love I'll praise, my gracious, patient God.
Must I be smitten, Lord? Are gentler measures vain?
Must I be smitten, Lord? Can nothing save but pain?

Thou trustedst me awhile; alas! I was deceived;
I revelled in the smile, yet to the dust I cleaved.
Then the fierce tempest broke—I knew from whom **it**
    came;
I read in that sharp stroke a Father's hand and name.

And yet I did Thee wrong; dark thoughts of Thee came
    in—

A forward, selfish throng—and I allowed the sin!
I did Thee wrong, my God; I wronged Thy truth and
    love;
I fretted at the rod—against Thy power I strove.

I said, my God, at length, this stormy heart remove;
Deny all other strength, but give me strength to love.
Come nearer, nearer still; let not Thy light depart;
Bend, break this stubborn will, dissolve this iron heart.

Less wayward let me be, more pliable and mild;
In glad simplicity more like a trustful child.
Less, less of self each day, and more, my God, of Thee;
O keep me in the way, however rough it be.

Less of the flesh each day, less of the world and sin;
More of Thy love, I pray; more of Thyself within.
Riper and riper now, each hour, let me become;
Less fit for scenes below—more fit for such a home.

More moulded to Thy will, Lord, let Thy servant be;
Higher and higher still, liker and liker Thee.
Leave naught that is unmeet; of all that is mine own
Strip me—and so complete my training of the throne.

O adorable Saviour! Thou who wast once Thyself a
pilgrim—the lonely, weary, homeless, afflicted One —
who hadst often no arm to lean upon, and no voice to
cheer Thee—an outcast wanderer and sojourner in
Thine own creation—I rejoice to think that Thou hast

trodden all this wilderness-world before me—that Thou knowest its dreariest paths. I take comfort in the assurance that there is, at the right hand of the Majesty on high, a fellow-sufferer who has drunk of every "brook by the way"—shed every tear of earthly sorrow— heaved every sigh of earthly suffering—and who, being himself the "tried and tempted One," is able and willing to succor every pilgrim who is tried and tempted, too.

—The Morning Watches.

The night is dark—behold the shade was deeper
In the still garden of Gethsemane,
When that calm voice awoke the weary sleeper,
"Couldst thou now watch one hour alone with me?"

O thou so weary of thy self-denials,
And so impatient of thy little cross,
Is it so hard to bear thy daily trials,
To count all earthly things a gainful loss?

What if thou always suffer'st tribulation,
What if thy Christian warfare never cease?
The gaining of the quiet habitation
Shall gather thee to everlasting peace.

Here are we all to suffer, walking lonely
The path that Jesus once Himself hath gone
Watch thou this hour in trustful patience only—
This one dark hour before the eternal dawn.

And He will come in His own time from heaven,
To set His earnest-hearted children free;
Watch only through this dark and painful even,
And the bright morning yet will break for thee.

Nearer, my God, to Thee!
Nearer to Thee!
E'en though it be a cross
That raiseth me;
Still all my song shall be,
Nearer, my God, to Thee,
Nearer to Thee.

Eternity! Eternity!
How long art thou, Eternity!
Who thinks on thee, to God will say,
Here strike, here wound, here judge, here slay,
Here let stern justice have her way—
Spare only in that endless day!

Full of trembling expectation,
Feeling much, and dreading more,
Mighty Lord of my salvation,
I Thy timely aid implore;

By thy suffering, O be near me,
All my suffering to sustain;
By Thy sorer griefs to cheer me,
By Thy more than mortal pain.

Call to mind that unknown anguish,
In the days of flesh below;
When Thy troubled soul did languish,
Under a whole world of woe.
When Thou didst our curse inherit,
Groan beneath our guilty load,
Burden'd with a wounded spirit,
Bruised beneath the hand of God.

By Thy dread, unknown temptation,
In that dark, satanic hour;
By Thy last, mysterious passion,
Screen me from the tempter's power;
By Thy fainting in the garden,
By Thy bloody sweat, I pray,
Write upon my heart Thy pardon,
Take my sins and fears away.

By the travail of Thy spirit,
By Thine outcry on the tree,
By Thine agonizing merit,
In my pangs remember me!
By Thy precious death assuring,
My poor dying soul befriend,
And with patience, all enduring,
Make me faithful to the end.

"REDEEMING THE TIME."

Lieutenant-Colonel Reuben Fletcher Harvey (2d Arkansas Regiment) was among the first to welcome me on my late mission to the army, and did more than any other to encourage the work which I had in hand. He could find enough, and more than enough, to exhaust his whole thought and attention in the duties of his station, and yet so circumspect was his walk, so consistent his example, so reverent his interest in the worship of God, and so earnest his efforts to promote the growth of virtue and holiness in all about him, that he seemed to be wholly occupied in "redeeming the time." At his own urgent request, and as a preparation for the terrible battle which was then in prospect,[2] he was admitted to the holy communion on the first Sunday in September. During the fearful fight which followed he was conspicuous for his proud and gallant carriage, freely exposing himself to the fiercest rage of the battle; but he moved unharmed through all, and seemed preserved for still further work on earth. God, however, needed him in a higher ministry; and a casual illness, aggravated and rendered fatal by his lofty, self-forgetful sense of duty, was the chosen instrument of his removal to a higher and better world.

The next, Jacob Kirby Brown, 5th Georgia Regiment, was one of ourselves—a child of the Church by birth and

---

[2] Chickamauga [A note original to the text.]

baptism. Amid the genial influences of home-life his better feelings were encouraged and his principles matured, and in the rite of confirmation he cheerfully owned his allegiance to the cause of Christ. His mild and amiable temper, his correct deportment, and his generous patriotism, all implied that he had caught the very spirit of the Church, and was becoming skilled in the rare accomplishment of wisely "redeeming the time." To such an [sic] one the place and mode of his promotion to an [sic] higher life could matter little; but God vouchsafed him what men call a glorious and honored departure. While nobly fighting to save from sacrilege and invasion the altar where he was wont to worship, and the home in which he was surrounded with so much purity and love, he fell unwarned, and yielded up his spirit without a struggle and without a pang.

The last, Lieutenant James Henry Foster (Yancey's Battalion Sharp-shooters), likewise a youth, was known and loved by many among you. His history, after his birth, begins where every child's history should begin, by the record of his baptism upon the register of his parish church. At a time when most young men think only of things fleeting and temporal, and take their tone from surrounding objects, he began to "redeem the time" by openly ratifying his baptismal vows, and accepting the place and portion of a child at his "Father's festal board." Upon the first approach of war he determined to exchange the peaceful surroundings of student-life for the din, and bustle, and danger of the tented field. It would postpone, if not prevent, the set settled purpose of his heart; it would separate him from a dear and delightful home; but, having formed the resolution, he never faltered. And, what chiefly concerns us now, he was enabled to maintain his interests in the cross, and preserve unbroken his Christian integrity, despite the dangers and temptations by which his pathway was beset. After he had bravely led his men in several attacks upon the foe, he fell, mortally wounded, in the act of encouraging another and more effective change. He had already learned to do and dare for his country and his God. He was now, as the crowning act of his earthly discipline, required to suffer and to wait. For a time the issue was doubtful. It was trying to a strong and active spirit, instinct with the hopes of ripening manhood, but he bore it all with meek submission. He would have desired to recover health and soundness; would fain perform a soldier's duty till his country should be free; would fain become a credit and protection in after years to the widowed mother who had so kindly and wisely guided his steps in childhood. But God willed otherwise— and what He willed was best for all. It was only left for the Christian soldier meekly to bow his head upon his breast, speak a calm farewell to those about him, and send a message, full of tenderness and pious counsel, to many a valued absent friend. This done, he quietly passed away, and entered the dark river wearing the serene and placid brow of a sleeping child. He has prudently "redeemed the time," exchanging the evil of its days for the happy years of eternity. He has crossed the threshold of a divine and heavenly life. He awaits in

Paradise the final welcome: "Enter thou into the joy of thy Lord."

In the face of such bright examples as these, and with our present access to all the means of grace and helps to holiness dispensed in the Church of Christ, let no one here complain, however evil be the days now passing, that he lacks ability to "walk circumspectly, redeeming the time."

Sermon— Rev. W. H. Clarke.

Listen! it is no dream; the Apostle's trump
Gives earnest of th' Archangel's; calmly now
   Our hearts yet beating high
   To that victorious lay.

Most like a warrior's to the mournful dirge
Of a true comrade, in the grave we trust
   Our treasure for a while;
   And if a tear steal down,

If human anguish o'er the shaded brow
Pass shuddering, when the handful of pure earth
   Touches the coffin lid;
   If, at our brother's name,

Once and again the thought, "for ever gone,"
Come o'er us like a cloud; yet, gentle spright,
   Thou turnest not away,
   Thou knowest us calm at heart.

One look, and we have seen our last of thee,
Till we, too, sleep, and our long sleep be o'er;
O cleanse us, ere we view
That countenance pure again.

Thou, who canst change our heart, and raise the dead,
As Thou art by to soothe our parting hour,
Be ready when we meet,
With Thy dear pardoning words.
—Lyra Apostolica.

A great sorrow recasts a soul; it either draws it nearer to
the friend whose intimacy must elevate it, or drives it
into the far cold space of rebellion and despair.
—Life Work.

O Thou who know'st our secret fame,
And every inmost grief,
In Thee I leave that long-lov'd name,
And find in Thee relief.
—Thoughts in Past Years.

Servant of God, well done;
Go forth from earth's employ;
The battle fought, the victory won,
Enter thy Master's joy.

The voice at midnight came,
He started up to hear;

A mortal arrow pierced his frame,
He fell—but felt no fear.

His sword was in his hand,
Still warm with recent fight,
Ready that moment, at command,
Through rock and steel to smite.

Oft with its fiery force
His arm had quelled the foe,
And laid, resistless, in his course,
The alien armies low.

Bent on such glorious toils,
The world to him was loss;
Yet all his trophies, all his spoils,
He hung upon the cross.

At midnight came the cry,
"To meet thy God prepare!"
He woke, and caught his Captain's eye;
Then strong in faith and prayer,

His spirit, with a bound,
Left its encumbering clay;
His tent, at sunrise, on the ground
A darkened ruin lay.

The pains of death are past,
Labor and sorrow cease;

And life's rough warfare closed at last,
His soul is formed in peace.

Soldier of Christ, well done!
Praise be thy new employ;
And while eternal ages run,
Rest in thy Saviour's joy.
—Montgomery.

THE HAPPINESS OF
A GLORIFIED SPIRIT.

Would you know where I am? I am at home in my Father's house, in the mansion prepared for me there. I am where I would be, where I have long and often desired to be; no longer on a stormy sea, but in a safe and quiet harbor. My working time is done, I am resting; my sowing time is done, I am reaping; my joy is as the joy of harvest. Would you know how it is with me? I am perfect in holiness; grace is swallowed up in glory; the top-stone of the building is brought forth. Would you know what I am doing? I see God; I see him as he is; not as through a glass darkly, but face to face; and the sight is transforming, it makes me like Him. I am in the sweet employment of my blessed Redeemer, my head husband, whom my soul loved, and for whose sake I was willing to part with all. I am here bathing myself at the springhead of heavenly pleasures and joys unutterable; and, therefore, weep not for me. I am here keeping a perpetual Sabbath; what that is, judge by your short Sabbath. I am here singing hallelujahs incessantly to Him who sits upon the throne, and rest not day or night from praising Him. Would you know what company I have? Blessed company— better than the best on earth; here are holy angels, and the spirits of just men made perfect. I am set down with Abraham, and Isaac, and Jacob, in the kingdom of God; with blessed Paul, and Peter, and James, and John, and all the

saints; and here I meet with many old acquaintances that I fasted and prayed with, who got before me hither. And, lastly, would you consider how long this is to continue? It is a garland that never withers; a crown of glory that fades not away; after millions of millions of ages, it will be as fresh as it is now; and, therefore, weep not for me.
—Matthew Henry.

'T is good that we should walk alone,
That we may so the readier own
The surer strength, our only stay
Along that shadowy way,
Which each alone must tread;
And o'er our path while sober even
Brings down the skies above our head,
May build the nobler hope that we may meet in heaven.
—Thoughts in Past Years.

Dear words! still let me read you o'er,
And on each heavenly accent pore;
"Come unto me," ye grief-opprest'!
Dear words, on you I rest;
Henceforth, I bow unto thy chastening rod,
And turn to thy dread cross, my Saviour and my God.
—Thoughts in Past Years.

He is as his country's friend Who cleanses his own heart from secret ill.

St. Luke xv, 17-24. —Let us observe the several degrees of a sinner's conversion and penitence. The first is, that he knows his misery and the corruption of his own heart; the second is, that he resolves to forsake sin and the occasion thereof. A man can not forsake them both too soon. The third degree is, when a sinner turns toward God, looks upon him as a father, entertains a desire to return to him, takes a resolution of doing it, and is convinced that he must not delay it. The fourth is, his making a confession of his sin, and beginning that confession by a name of love, "my Father;" because the love of God is the foundation of all true repentance. The chief motive to the hatred of sin is because it is contrary to the goodness of God, and because He, who is the best of all fathers, is offended thereby. The fifth is, his humbling himself as being altogether unworthy of the grace and mercy of God. It is love, and the spirit of adoption, which gives us a right to call God our Father. The acknowledgement of our own unworthiness is an acceptance of the humiliation which is due to the sinner. God pours into the heart of true penitents so much comfort and delight as inspires them with a holy confidence of the pardon of their sins and reconciliation.

In the next place, the sinner openly owns his sin, and bears the shame of his ingratitude. The more a penitent humbles himself, the higher does God raise him, and heap upon him greater benefits. To the grace of reconciliation, God adds abundance of other graces, with which He covers the nakedness of a converted sinner, clothing him with Jesus Christ, His righteousness, His merits, His virtues. He seals this new covenant with a lively impression of His Spirit, which is the seal of adoption, a pledge of the inheritance in heaven, and an earnest of the eternal promises. He gives him such graces and assistances as enable him to walk in the way of His commandments, and in the practice of good works. He must not live either to the world, or to sin, which gave him death, or to himself; but he must live to Him who was made man on purpose to seek him, and who died to raise him to life. Let his life, therefore, be one continued act of thanksgiving.

—Quesnel.

"I am not good enough; I feel so unworthy." Remember that a sense of unworthiness is the first thing that makes us worthy in the sight of God. "The publican standing afar off, would not so much as lift up his eyes to heaven, but smote upon his breast, saying, God be merciful to me, a sinner." Think over the story of the prodigal son. When he "came to himself," his only plea was his unworthiness; for he said, "I will arise and go to my father, and will say to him, Father, I have sinned against heaven, and before thee, and am no more worthy to be called thy son: make me as one of thy hired servants."

In my hand no price I bring,
Simply to Thy cross I cling.

Him that cometh unto me I will in nowise cast out.
[John 6:37]

Just as I am—without one plea,
But that thy blood was shed for me,
And that thou bid'st me come to thee,
O Lamb of God, I come.

Just as I am—and waiting not
To rid my soul of one dark blot—
To Thee whose blood can cleanse such spot,
O Lamb of God, I come.

Just as I am—though tossed about
With many a conflict, many a doubt,
With fears within, and foes without—
O Lamb of God, I come.

Just as I am—poor, wretched, blind—
Sight, riches, healing of the mind,
Yea, all I need, in thee to find,
O Lamb of God, I come.

Just as I am—thy love unknown
Has broken every barrier down:
Now to be thine, yea, thine alone,
O Lamb of God, I come.
　　—Charlotte Elliott.

Now, when they heard this, they were pricked in their heart, and said unto Peter and to the rest of the apostles: Men and brethren, what shall we do?

Then Peter said unto them, repent and be baptized every one of you, in the name of Jesus Christ, for the remission of sins, and ye shall receive the gift of the Holy Ghost.

For the promise is unto you, and to your children, and to all that are afar off, even as many as the Lord our God shall call.
—Acts ii, 37-39.

And now why tarriest thou? Arise, and be baptized and wash away thy sins, calling on the name of the Lord.
—Acts xxii, 16.

As many of you as have been baptized into Christ have put on Christ. [Galatians 3:27.]

There is a sign upon my brow,
The sign of suffering love—
Upon me rests a sacred vow,
'T is register'd above;
And should my faithless heart repine,
At grief and suffering now,
Then I will think upon that sign,
And that baptismal vow;

And it shall stir His strength within,
Whose name is named on me,
Through whom the victory I may win,
And more than conqueror be;
And I will go and kneel apart,
And clasp my hands in prayer,
Until He nerve my coward heart,
The daily cross to bear.

The swift may stumble in the race,
The strong in battle fail,
But they who ever seek Thy face
Shall in Thy might prevail.
And, oh! when on each brow shall shine,
Thy gift a fadeless crown,
What joy to own the glory Thine,
And lowly cast it down!

God can affix and join His blessings and helps to whatever He pleases. By His appointment the common waters of Jordan healed Naaman, the Syrian. By His appointment a brazen serpent healed all those that were bitten, only looking upon it with faith in God's commandments. By the very shadow of St. Peter many, we are assured, were healed of their diseases.

And here (St. Mark vi, 56) as many as touched our Saviour's garments were made whole.

And it is thus that the two sacraments became means of salvation to all such as receive them.

The water in baptism, with the blessing and grace of God, has power in it to cleanse us from our sins.

And the bread in the Lord's Supper being set apart and blessed, becometh that bread that nourisheth to eternal life.
—Bishop Wilson.

Soldiers of Christ, arise!
And put your armor on,
Strong in the strength which God supplies,
Through His eternal Son.

Strong in the Lord of hosts,
And in His mighty power;
Who in the strength of Jesus trusts,
Is more than conqueror.

Stand then in His great might,
With all his strength endued;
And take, to arm you for the fight,
The panoply of God.

That having all things done,
And all your conflicts past,
Ye may behold your victory won,
And stand complete at last.
—Hymn.

Thy vows are upon me, O God. I will render praises unto
Thee. [Psalm 56:12.]

CONFIRMATION; OR THE LAYING OF HANDS.

O happy day that stays my choice
On Thee, my Saviour and my God;
Well may this glowing heart rejoice,
And tell Thy goodness all abroad.
—Hymn.

Now when the apostles which were at Jerusalem heard
that Samaria had received the word of God, they sent
unto them Peter and John, who, when they were come
down, prayed for them that they might receive the Holy
Ghost;

For as yet He was fallen upon none of them: only they
were baptized in the name of the Lord Jesus.

Then laid they their hands on them, and they received the
Holy Ghost.
—Acts viii, 14-17.

Draw, Holy Ghost, Thy sevenfold veil
Between us and the fires of youth;
Breathe, Holy Ghost, Thy freshening gale,
Our fevered brow in age to soothe.

And oft as sin and sorrow tire,
The hallow'd hour do Thou renew,
When beckon'd up the awful choir
By pastoral hand, toward Thee we drew;

When, trembling at the sacred rail,
We hid our eyes and held our breath,
Felt Thee how strong, our hearts how frail,
And longed to own Thee to the death.

For ever on our souls be trac'd
That blessing dear, that dove-like hand,
A sheltering rock in memory's waste,
O'ershadowing all the weary land.

TURN
YOU TO THE
STRONGHOLD, YE
PRISONERS OF HOPE.
—ZECH. IX, 12.

Though the bolts are not drawn across the door; though your windows are not barred, yet what bolts or bars could hold you faster than your sickness. Your house is your prison, or your room in the hospital is a cell in the prison; and you yourself are a prisoner of God. Now, in order to profit by your imprisonment, consider first this one great truth, which is revealed to your senses in this your sickness. You are not your own, but God's. As long as you were well, you may have felt yourself to be your own; you may have gone where you liked, and done what you liked; but now you must needs feel that you are not your own; you have no power over yourself; you are in God's hands, and you can not resist Him; you are His altogether; your body is His, and your soul is His; you are a witness to yourself of God's power. He is Lord indeed; you are not your own. Well, then, if you are His, He can do with you what He likes; He is now doing what He likes; He likes at present to make you sick, to cause you to suffer, to give you a cup of trembling;

He is not consulting your likings, or your pleasure; He is going against your likings, and He has his way. He is now teaching you what you have so frequently forgotten— first, that you belong entirely to Him; next, that you contain in yourself great power and capacity of suffering, which, by His Almighty power, might be heightened and lengthened in another world beyond all our powers of conception.

But there is wonderful love in his teachings. Had he given you over, had He ceased to care for you, had He felt no love toward your soul, He would have left you to drift on to destruction. He would not have taught you any lessons in godliness; He would have let you take your own way, and then taken vengeance if you went wrong. But because He wishes you well, He has laid upon your bed that He might plead with you by His spirit. He has taken you by force from the cares, the trials, and pleasures of the world in which you were too much entangled, that He might speak to your soul, and argue with you for good.

He has made time for you to think, because you would not make time for yourself. He gives you pain to humble you, and to convince you of sin, and to make you feel the terrors of the Lord. Everything is prepared for you that you may think; your heart is softened, now that the world is removed from you; your conscience is not deafened by the noises of the world, nor clamored down; it can make itself heard now; now that the noise of the battle is hushed, the "still small voice" can be heard; you are, somehow or other, you know not how, in a more solemn and serious mood, and incline more to the thing of God. Yes, you are under the blessed discipline of the cross. The cross is laid on you; mercy has put this burden on your flesh; your Saviour comes to you in suffering; He who once suffered in the flesh comes to sufferers; He draws near to the sick. His Holy Spirit is in sick-rooms; sickness is the soul's medicine—bitter, yet yielding sweetness. He would not destroy you, for He has died for you. He would not cast that body into hell, as it is His twice over— once by creation, again by redemption. He desires to save it; therefore, He makes it sick.

Look, then, in this way upon your sickness; receive it as you would receive an angel; take it as medicine for the soul from the hand of the Lord. But if you desire to make your illness fulfill its end, let me give you this counsel, which may help you to turn it to good account.

Examine yourself strictly; sit as a judge on your whole past life, beginning with your youth, and tracing the stream up to the present hour. Search and try your ways, and call them to remembrance; so shall you be the better able to turn away from sin to the testimonies of the Lord. Do this not lightly, but reverently and soberly, as in the presence of the great Judge of heaven and earth, before whose dread tribunal you must certainly appear at the day of judgment to give an account of all your actions.

Examine your life and conversation by the rule of God's commandments, and whereinsoever you shall perceive yourself to have offended, either by will, word or deed, there to bewail your own sinfulness, and to confess yourself to Almighty God with full purpose of amendment of life; and if you shall perceive your offenses to be such as are not only against God, but also against your neighbors, then you shall reconcile yourself unto them—being ready to make restitution and satisfaction, according to the uttermost of your powers, for all injuries and wrongs done by you to any other, and being likewise ready to forgive others who have offended you, as you would have forgiveness of your offences at God's hand.

Endeavor, at once, to bring forth fruits of repentance. You may say, "What can I do while I lie on a sick-bed?" You may do much. Lie there, for instance, without repining or murmuring; bear pain patiently; be meek and uncomplaining; be not selfish nor irritable; be gentle and considerate toward those who watch you, and wait on you; be thankful for all kind services of friends or attendants. This is one way in which you can bring forth the fruit of repentance. There are trials of patience, and of temper, of endurance of pain on your sick-bed. Take your pain and your confinement to bed, and your long days and restless nights as punishments which you deserve; take them meekly and thankfully, as from the Lord's hand. This is one way in which you can show your sorrow for sin.

Of course, that is not to be called repentance which is not followed by an altered life; but you can show the beginning of an altered life while you lie upon your bed. If you have been worldly, you can try to be unworldly; if you have been selfish, you can try to be unselfish; if you have been proud, you can try to be meek; if you have neglected to pray, you can learn to pray; if you have any quarrels; you have done wrong to any one, you can confess, and ask forgiveness.

It is very profitable to meditate upon the sufferings and passions of Christ when we are in pain, for we shall get deeper views of our own sinfulness, and of His unspeakable love who chose those sufferings—who willingly took them upon Him, who had it in His power to refuse the suffering. We also learn patience under our pains, by His example of patience; and it gives us comfort to think that our Lord, by His human suffering, is brought near to us, and, having experienced what we feel, is "touched with a feeling of our infirmities," and enters into our sorrows. In His pains, we have a pledge that He will pity and succor us in ours.

Resign yourself at once into the hands of God, seeking in all ways to be at peace with Him—that, whether you live, you may live unto the Lord; or, whether you die, you may die unto the Lord; that, living or dying, you may be the Lord's. And now I pray that the God of peace may give you His peace in your time of sickness, and, by His Spirit, turn it to the good of your body and soul, that you may be saved in the day of the Lord, and may be numbered with the saints in glory everlasting, for our Lord Jesus Christ's sake.

The word of God, as the Psalmist speaks, "is perfect and pure, converting the soul, rejoicing the heart, and enlightening the eyes; yea, sweeter than honey, and more to be desired than the purest gold."

Let God's word, then, be your companion in sickness.

The following selections from Holy Scripture may be added at the morning and evening prayer.

	MORNING	EVENING.
* SUNDAY	Isaiah xxxviii	2 Corinth. v.
* MONDAY	Lamentations iii	St. Luke xvi.
* TUESDAY	Job xiv	St. John xi.
* WEDNESDAY	Isaiah xxvi	St. Luke xv.
* THURSDAY	Eccles. xi. and xii	St. James iv.
* FRIDAY	Isaiah lxiv	1 St. Peter i.
* SATURDAY	Malachi iii	St. Matthew xxv.

Or—

	MORNING	EVENING.
* SUNDAY	Isaiah lxv	1 Corinth. xv.
* MONDAY	Job vii	Romans viii.
* TUESDAY	Job ii to v. 11	1 Thess. iv&ch. v.

* WEDNESDAY	Isaiah lii	John xvii.
* THURSDAY	Isaiah lv	Hebrews xii.
* FRIDAY	Isaiah xl	Philippians iii.
* SATURDAY	Job xxxiii	John xiv.

In selecting these lessons a task is not attempted to be imposed, but merely appropriate portions of Holy Scripture pointed out, to be used as weakness and circumstances allow.

MORNING PRAYER.

Almighty and most merciful Father; I have erred, and strayed from Thy ways like a lost sheep. I have followed too much the devices and desires of my own heart. I have offended against Thy holy laws. I have left undone those things which I ought to have done; and I have done those things which I ought not to have done; and there is no health in me. But Thou, O Lord, have mercy upon me, a miserable offender. Spare Thou those, O God, who confess their faults. Restore Thou those who are penitent; according to Thy promises declared unto mankind in Christ Jesus our Lord. And grant, O most merciful Father, for His sake, that I may hereafter live a godly, righteous, and sober life, to the glory of Thy holy name. Amen.

Our Father, who art in heaven, hallowed be Thy name. Thy kingdom come. Thy will be done on earth, as it is in heaven. Give us this day our daily bread. Forgive us our trespasses, as we forgive those who trespass against us. And lead us not into temptation; but deliver us from evil: for Thine is the kingdom, and the power, and the glory, for ever and ever. Amen.

Then repeat:

I BELIEVE in God the Father Almighty, Maker of heaven and earth: And in Jesus Christ, His only Son, our Lord; Who was conceived by the Holy Ghost; Born of the Virgin Mary; Suffered under Pontius Pilate; Was crucified, dead, and buried; He descended into hell;*

(*He descended into hell, or He went into the place of departed spirits, which are considered words of the same meaning in the Creed.)

The third day He rose from the dead; He ascended into heaven; And sitteth on the right hand of God the Father Almighty; From thence He shall come to judge the quick and the dead.

I believe in the Holy Ghost; The holy Catholic Church; The Communion of Saints; The Forgiveness of Sins; The Resurrection of the body; And the Life everlasting. Amen.

After which, say:

I am Thy prisoner, O Lord, chained by sickness to a bed of pain; but let me not fret, even because I am Thine; Thine, whose chain I can not break; Thine, who dost draw me to Thee by this chain; Thine, who for my sins dost justly bind me; Thine, who knowest when it is best to loose me; Thine, who hearest every groan within me; Thine, who for my sins mightest bind me in everlasting chains, and sendest this sickness to save me. O Lord, since I am so many ways Thine, let me submit to Thy chain, and lie as Thy prisoner and Thy patient before Thee; and let Thy pity, in Thy good time, release me, for Jesus Christ's sake. Amen.

Remember not, Lord, my offences, nor the offences of my forefathers; neither take Thou vengeance of my sins; spare me, good Lord; spare Thy people whom Thou hast redeemed with Thy most precious blood, and be not angry with us for ever.

By the mystery of Thy Holy Incarnation; by Thy Holy Nativity and Circumcision; by Thy Baptism, Fasting, and Temptation;

Good Lord deliver me.

By Thine Agony and Bloody Sweat; by Thy Cross and Passion; by Thy precious Death and Burial; by Thy glorious Resurrection and Ascension; and by the coming of the Holy Ghost,

Good Lord, deliver me.

In all time of my tribulation; in all time of my prosperity; in the hour of death, and in the day of judgment,

Good Lord, deliver me.

O Lamb of God, that takest away the sins of the world;

Grant me Thy peace.

O Lamb of God, who takest away the sins of the world;

Have mercy upon me.

God the Father bless me, God the Son defend me, God the Holy Ghost preserve me and all mine and His, now and evermore.

Amen.

THE COMFORTABLE WORDS.

Hear what comfortable words our Saviour Christ saith unto all who truly turn to Him:

"Come unto me, all ye that travail and are heavy laden, and I will refresh you."
 —St. Matt. xi, 28.

So God loved the world, that He gave His only begotten Son, to the end that all that believe in Him should not perish, but have everlasting life.
—St. John iii, 16.

Hear also what Saint Paul saith:

"This is a true saying, and worthy of all men to be received, that Christ Jesus came into the world to save sinners."
—1 Tim. i, 15.

Here also what Saint John saith:

"If any man sin, we have an Advocate with the Father, Jesus Christ the Righteous; and He is the propitiation for our sins."
—1 St. John ii, 1,2.

EVENING PRAYER.

Almighty God, Father of our Lord Jesus Christ, Maker of all things, Judge of all men; I acknowledge and bewail my manifold sins and wickedness, which I, from time to time, most grievously have committed, by thought, word, and deed, against Thy Divine Majesty, provoking most justly Thy wrath and indignation against me. I do earnestly repent, and am heartily sorry for these my misdoings; the remembrance of them is grievous unto me; the burden of them is intolerable. Have mercy upon me, most merciful Father; for thy Son our Lord Jesus Christ's sake, forgive me all that is past; and grant that I may ever hereafter serve and please Thee in newness of life, to the honor and glory of Thy name, through Jesus Christ our Lord. Amen.

Almighty God, the Father of our Lord, Jesus Christ, who desirest not the death of a sinner, but that he may turn from his wickedness and live; and hast promised pardon to them that truly repent and unfeignedly believe Thy Holy Gospel; of Thy mercy I beseech Thee grant me true repentance and Thy Holy Spirit, that those things may please Thee which I do at this present, and that the rest of my life hereafter may be pure and holy, so that at the last I may come to Thine eternal joy, through Jesus Christ, our Lord. Amen.

O MOST mighty God and merciful Father, who hast compassion upon all men, and hatest nothing that Thou hast made; who wouldest not the death of a sinner, but rather that he should turn from his sin and be saved; mercifully forgive my trespasses; receive and comfort me, grieved and wearied with the burden of my sins. Thy property is always to have mercy; to Thee only it appertaineth to forgive sins. Spare me, therefore, good Lord, spare me whom Thou hast redeemed; enter not into judgment with Thy servant, who is vile earth, and a miserable sinner; but so turn Thine anger from me, who meekly acknowledge my vileness, and truly repent me of my faults, and so make haste to help me in this world, that I may ever live with Thee in the world to come; through Jesus Christ, our Lord. Amen.

Lord, lift Thou up the light of Thy countenance upon me; and in all the pains of my body, in all the agonies of my spirit, let Thy comforts refresh my soul, and enable me patiently to wait till my change come. And grant, O Lord, that when my earthly house of this tabernacle is dissolved, I may have a building of God, a house not made with hands, eternal in the heavens; through Him who by His precious blood hath purchased it for me, Jesus Christ, our Redeemer. Amen.

Our Father, who art in heaven, hallowed be Thy name. Thy kingdom come. Thy will be done on earth, as it is in heaven. Give us this day our daily bread. And forgive us

our trespasses, as we forgive those who trespass against us.
And lead us not into temptation. But deliver us from evil.
For thine is the kingdom, and the power, and the glory,
for ever and ever. Amen.

O Sun of Righteousness, keep me from utter darkness; let
me so sleep in Thy peace, that I may be ever ready to arise
and meet Thee in Thy glory. Amen. Amen.

Rock of Ages, cleft for me,
Let me hide myself in Thee;
Let the water and the blood,
From Thy side a healing flood,
Be of sin the double cure,
Save from wrath, and make me pure.

PRAYERS WHICH MAY BE ADDED TO THE MORNING AND EVENING DEVOTIONS.

FOR TRUST IN GOD.

O Almighty God, our only help in time of trouble, who never failest them that trust in Thee: grant me grace, I beseech Thee, at all times, and in all my difficulties and distresses, so to put my whole trust and confidence in Thee, that I may cast all my care upon Thee, and with cheerfulness submit myself to Thy hands; give me, in this the hour of trial, to rely upon Thee, through the merits of my Redeemer, knowing assuredly that all things shall work together for good to them that love Thee. And, O Lord, however Thou art pleased to deal with my body, yet spare my soul, I beseech Thee, and deliver it from the bitter pains of eternal death. O take me not out of this world until Thou hast fitted me in some measure for Thy heavenly kingdom. Grant, O Lord, that, whether I live, I may live unto Thee; or, whether I die, I may die unto Thee; so that, living and dying, I may be Thine, through Jesus Christ, my ever blessed Saviour and Redeemer. Amen.

IN THE PROSPECT OF AN OPERATION.

Jesus, my Redeemer, my Saviour, Thou who didst not despise the Cross, but didst yield Thyself to the tormentors, who didst drink of the cup of sorrow willingly, yet didst taste of its bitterness, be Thou with me in the hour of my agony; strengthen me to bear all that shall be laid upon me; in every pang may my spirit still have power to say with Thee, not my will, but Thine, be done.

Give me grace, O Lord, to yield up my will into Thy hands; to trust in Thee in Thy might, and in Thy providence, rather than in the skill of man. Do Thou bless it, Lord, if so it seemeth good in Thy sight, for my relief; but if not, if it should be in vain, let me still bless and praise Thee, and submit myself to Thy good pleasure. Let me go to this trial in the strength of the Lord God committing myself to Him that judgeth righteously; all which I ask in His name who is touched with our infirmities, Jesus Christ, Thy blessed Son. Amen.

FOR THE FEAR OF GOD.

O Gracious Lord, who only art high and to be feared, fill my soul with a holy awe and reverence of Thee, that I may give Thee the honor due unto Thy name, and so esteem all things which relate to Thee that I may never profane what Thou hast made holy and set apart for Thyself. And, O Lord, since Thou art a God who will by no means clear the guilty, let the dread of Thy displeasure, and the fear of Thy judgment, and the sentence of the last day, make me tremble to provoke Thee in anything. O let me not so misplace my fear, that I may be afraid of any man and forget Thee, the Lord, my Maker, and my Judge, but replenish my soul with that fear of the Lord which is the beginning of wisdom, and which may keep me in a constant conformity to Thy holy will. Hear me, O Lord, I beseech Thee, and put this fear in my heart, that I may never depart from Thee, but may, with fear and trembling, work out my salvation; through Jesus Christ, our Lord. Amen.

FOR CONTRITION.

O most merciful God, who, notwithstanding my con-tinued abuses of Thy goodness, and my unthankfulness of Thy long-suffering and patience toward me, vouchsafest to continue to me the means of grace and repentance; awaken my soul from the sleep of death, and make me duly sensible of the greatness of my transgressions, and of the dreadful eternity of torments to which, without repentance, they must consign me. Give me a deep contrition for having offended Thee, my merciful Creator and Redeemer. O work in my soul that godly sorrow which leadeth to repentance unto salvation: that, heartily detesting and loathing all my past abominations, and begging at Thy feet for pardon with strong crying and tears, I may obtain mercy of Thee, who despisest not the sighing of a contrite heart, for the merits and intercession of Thy beloved Son, Jesus Christ, our Lord. Amen.

FOR PARDON.

O Eternal and most gracious Father, I cast down my soul before Thee. O cast me not away from Thee. I can not stand at the bar of Thy justice; I therefore lie down at the footstool of Thy mercy. I condemn myself for my sins; Lord, judge me not. O my God, hear the prayers and cries of a sinner who calls earnestly for mercy. Blot out my sins in the blood of my Saviour. Though red as crimson, Thou has promised the penitent they shall be as snow; O pardon this guilty soul of mine, I beseech Thee. Wash me from my sins and forgive all mine iniquities. And let Thy Holy Spirit assist and strengthen me to overcome my temptations, for the blessed merits of Him who overcame the world for me, Thy dear Son, Jesus Christ, our Lord. Amen.

FOR SINCERITY.

O holy Lord, who searchest the heart and triest the reins; try me, I beseech Thee, and seek the ground of my heart; purge it from all hypocrisy and insincerity, and suffer not any accursed thing to lurk within me; give me truth in the inward parts, and purity of heart, that I may be prepared to see Thee in Thy kingdom, through Jesus Christ our Lord. Amen.

FOR HUMILITY.

Almighty God, who resisteth the proud, and giveth grace to the humble; mercifully grant that I may follow the example of the great humility of Thy blessed Son, who did humble Himself to take upon Him our flesh, and to suffer death upon the cross; convince me that I am less than the least of all Thy mercies; that as I am vile in myself, so let me be vile in mine own eyes, and may therefore esteem every man better than myself. Grant this, O Father, for Thy Son Jesus Christ's sake. Amen.

FOR FAITH.

O blessed Lord, whom without faith it is impossible to please, let Thy Spirit, I beseech Thee, work in me such a faith as may be acceptable in Thy sight, even such as may show itself by my works, that it may enable me to overcome the world, and conform me to the image of the Christ on whom I believe; that so, at the last, I may receive the end of my faith, even the salvation of my soul, by the same Jesus Christ our Lord. Amen.

FOR HOPE.

O Lord, who art the hope of all the ends of the earth, let me never be destitute of a well-grounded hope, nor yet possessed with a vain presumption; suffer me not to think Thou wilt either be reconciled to my sins or reject my repentance; but give me, I beseech Thee, such a hope as may both encourage and enable me to purify myself, even as Thou art pure, that when Thou shalt appear I may be made like unto Thee, in Thy eternal and glorious kingdom, where, with the Father and the Holy Ghost, Thou livest and reignest one God, world without end. Amen.

PRAYERS TO BE USED BY THE FRIENDS OR ATTENDANTS OF THE SICK.

When there appeareth but small hope of recovery.

O Father of mercies, and the God of all comfort, our only help in time of need; we fly unto Thee for succor in behalf of this Thy servant, here lying under Thy hand in great weakness of body. Look graciously upon him, O Lord; and the more the outward man decayeth, strengthen him, we beseech Thee, so much the more continually with Thy grace and Holy Spirit in the inner man. Give him unfeigned repentance for all the errors of his life past, and steadfast faith in Thy Son Jesus; that his sins may be done away by Thy mercy, and his pardon sealed in heaven before he go hence and be no more seen. We know, O Lord, that there is no word impossible with Thee; and that, if Thou wilt, Thou canst even yet raise him up, and grant him a longer continuance amongst us; yet forasmuch as in all appearance the time of his dissolution draweth near, so fit and prepare him, we beseech Thee, against the hour of death, that after his departure hence in peace, and in Thy favor, his soul may be received into Thine everlasting kingdom; through the merits and mediation of Jesus Christ, Thine only Son, our Lord and Saviour. Amen.

THE MANNER OF COMMENDING THE
SICK INTO THE HANDS OF GOD AT
THE HOUR OF DEATH.

God the Father, who hath created thee, God the Son, who hath redeemed thee, God the Holy Ghost, who hath infused His grace into thee, be now and evermore thy defense, assist thee in this thy last trial, and bring thee into the way of everlasting life. Amen.

Into Thy merciful hands, O heavenly Father, we commend the soul of Thy servant now departing; acknowledge, we beseech Thee, a sheep of Thine own fold, a lamb of Thine own flock. Receive him into the arms of Thy mercy, into the sacred rest of everlasting peace, and into the glorious estate of Thy chosen saints in heaven. O Father Almighty, receive and forgive. O Holy Ghost the Comforter, comfort him in the dark valley of the shadow of death. O Saviour of the world, who by Thy cross and precious blood hast redeemed him, save and help this Thy departing servant, O Lord. Amen.

The only feast of which a sick man is wise to partake, is that

*"Sacred feast, which Jesus makes,
Rich banquet of His flesh and blood."
—Hymn.

*The place was bright
"With something of celestial light"—
A simple Altar by the bed
For high Communion meetly spread,
Chalice, and plate, and snowy vest.—
We ate and drank: then calmly blest,
All mourners, one with dying breath,
We sate and talk'd of Jesus' death.
—Christian Year.

MEDITATIONS UPON RECOVERY.

If God hath of His mercy heard thy prayers, and restored thee to thy health again, consider, with thyself—

1. That thou hast now received from God, as it were, another life; spend it, therefore, to the honor of God, in newness of life; let thy sin die with thy sickness, but live thou by grace to holiness.

2. Put not off the thought of the day of death, for thou knowest not for all this how near it is at hand; and being so fairly warned, be wiser. For, if thou be taken in an unprepared state the next time, thy excuse will be less and thy judgment greater.

3. Fulfill all your vows of holier living, of more frequent and abundant alms-giving, of more constant public worship, and of more faithful self-examination.

The highest act of worship in which a Christian can join is the Holy Communion of Christ's Body and Blood; neglect not, then, this privilege, so soon as you are sufficiently recovered.

4. In all things give thanks unto God. Pray without ceasing; increase your prayers at home and be more devout in church. Keep God in all your thoughts; enter on your worldly labors with a devout spirit; prepare daily for the great day of Christ, that you may be found watching at His coming, and may be numbered among the saints in glory everlasting.

DEVOTIONS.

I will magnify Thee, O Lord, for Thou hast set me up: and not made my foes to triumph over me.
O Lord I cried unto Thee: and Thou hast healed me. [Psalm 30:1–2]

Thou hast turned my heaviness into joy: Thou hast put off my sackcloth, and girded me with gladness.

The Lord hath chastened and corrected me, but He hath not given me over unto death. [Psalm 118:18]

I will pay Thee my vows, O God, which my lips have uttered, and my mouth hath spoken when I was in trouble. [Psalm 66:13–14]

O Lord, I give Thee humble and hearty thanks for Thy great mercy in bringing me back from the grave. What Thou hast further for me to do or to suffer, Thou alone knowest: Lord, give me patience and courage, and all Christian resolution and grace to do Thee service. And now that Thou hast mercifully restored me, let me live to love, to honor, and to obey Thee, and all this through Jesus Christ. Amen.

O Almighty God, I give Thee humble thanks, for that Thou hast vouchsafed to deliver me from the pains and perils of my late sickness; grant, I beseech Thee, most merciful Father, that I, through Thy help, may both faithfully live and walk according to Thy will in this life present, and also may be a partaker of everlasting glory in the life to come, through Jesus Christ our Lord. Amen.

I praise Thee, I worship Thee, I glorify Thee, I give thanks to Thee, O Lord God, Lamb of God, Son of the Father, that takest away the sins of the world. For Thou only art holy, Thou only art the Lord; Thou only, O Christ, with the Holy Ghost, art most high in the glory of God the Father. Holy, holy, holy, Lord God of Hosts, heaven and earth are full of Thy glory: for these and all Thy mercies, glory be to Thee, O Lord Most High. Amen.

Be patient! O be patient! Put your ear against the earth;
Listen there how noiselessly the germ o' the seed has birth—

How noiselessly and gently it upheaves its little way
Till it parts the scarcely broken ground, and the blade
stands up in the day.

Be patient! O be patient! the germs of mighty thought
Must have their silent undergrowth, must underground
be wrought;
But as sure as there's a power that makes the grass appear,
Our land shall be green with liberty, the blade-time shall
be here.
—Dean Trench.

"THY WILL BE DONE."

My God, my Father, while I stray,
Far from my home, in life's rough way,
O teach me from my heart to say,
"Thy will be done."

Though dark my path, and sad my lot,
Let me be still and murmur not,
Or breathe the prayer divinely taught,
"Thy will be done."

What though in lonely grief I sigh,
For friends beloved, no longer nigh,
Submissive would I still reply,
"Thy will be done."

If Thou should'st call me to resign,
What most I prize, it ne'er was mine;
I only yield Thee what is Thine;
"Thy will be done."

Let but my fainting heart be blest
With Thy sweet Spirit for its guest;
My God, to Thee I leave the rest;
"Thy will be done."

Renew my will from day to day,
Blend it with Thine, and take away
All that now makes it hard to say,
"Thy will be done." Amen.

"LORD, REMEMBER ME."

O Thou, from Whom all goodness flows,
I lift my soul to Thee;
In all my sorrows, conflicts, woes,
Good Lord, remember me.

If on my aching, burdened heart,
My sins lie heavily,
Thy pardon grant, Thy peace impart;
Good Lord, remember me.

If trials sore obstruct my way,
And ills I can not flee,
Then let my strength be as my day;
Good Lord, remember me.

If, worn with pain, disease, and grief,
This feeble frame should be,
Grant patience, rest, and kind relief;
Good Lord remember me.

And oh! when, in the hour of death,
I bow to Thy decree,
Jesu, receive my parting breath;
Good Lord, remember me. Amen.

www.ingramcontent.com/pod-product-compliance
Lightning Source LLC
Chambersburg PA
CBHW020156090426
42734CB00008B/841